THE
MYSTERIES
OF GOD

REVISED EDITION

THE MYSTERIES OF GOD, REVISED EDITION
By H.A. Ironside. Revised by J. Kalmbach.

Published by Jason Kalmbach *(publishing@jasonkalmbach.com)*
Markham, ON, Canada.

All Scripture quotations are from the World English Bible British Edition (2017) (unless otherwise noted) which is not copyrighted and in the public domain.

ISBN 978-1-7751846-2-1 Paperback

Contents

Introduction

WHEN I unintentionally came across a decades–old copy of the original version of this volume by H.A. Ironside during a weekend away, it captured my attention so fully, I ended up reading it all the way through before I headed home. Not that I was entirely unacquainted with the topic, but I was impressed by the great preacher's ability to both thoroughly and concisely expound the important (and tragically, mostly ignored) Biblical subject of the New Testament mystery doctrines.

I find myself in agreement with both the original author and the Apostle Paul who desired that Christian believers not be ignorant of these significant and glorious truths. The original text of this book is believed to be in the public domain, and is freely available, but uses antiquated language and out-of-date cultural references. This revision was undertaken not to change or improve the content in any major way, but to update an influential writing that is now over a century old, in an effort to make this insightful teaching and commentary more accessible and understandable to a modern audience.

It is my prayer that a new generation of believers will grow in grace and knowledge from this work, and that the Lord may receive all glory. — *J. Kalmbach*

Original Preface

KNOWING of nothing that aims to present in one volume, the various mysteries of the New Testament, it has been a happy service to pen these papers, hoping thereby to minister to the profit of some who, while of the household of faith, may have given little or no attention to truths of such vast importance.

The teaching set forth is not original with the writer. He is indebted to many, both through oral and written ministry, for most of the instruction he now seeks to impart to others. May it be yours, reader, to test all by the word of the living God, and thus find true profit. — *H. A. Ironside*

CHAPTER 1

The Secret Things

*A*s he finishes instructing the children of Israel, in the plains of Moab, Moses said, "the secret things belong to the LORD our God; but the things that are revealed belong to us and to our children forever, that we may do all the words of this law." [1]

This Bible passage is often completely misapplied and inappropriately used by overcautious souls to deter inquiring ones from delving into the deep things of God. That was never the intention. When the great lawgiver Moses spoke those words, the *'things that are revealed'* consisted of the covenant the Lord had just established, together with the records Moses had already made by the inspiration of God in the first four books of our Bibles. *'The secret things'* however, were God's purposes of grace which He was about to reveal upon the demonstration of their utter failure, and their inability to claim anything on the basis of the law, which they had broken right from the start. All their rights were forfeited. But God had provisions of grace yet to be shown. He had infinite resources in Himself, to be displayed when they were forced to admit that theirs were insufficient.

God's revelation of His purpose has been gradual. In the Old Testament, two special entities were promised—the woman's Offspring, and the offspring of Abraham. Through the former, the latter were to be blessed, and be a blessing to all the nations of the earth. The testimony of the prophets does not go any further beyond this.

---

[1] Deut. 29:29

As in Moses' day, so too in the days of Malachi (the last of the Old Testament prophets, before the coming of John, the one who would prepare the way of Messiah) there were *'secret things'* which the time had not yet come to make known.

The English phrase *'secret things'* in Deuteronomy 29:29 is a translation of *'sathar'* in the Hebrew, which scholars define as things which are *hidden*. Please note that it does not refer to things too high for human understanding, as it is often assumed to mean, but rather it simply means things that are concealed, which cannot be known unless disclosed to us by God.

In the Septuagint[2] the translators chose the word *'krupta'*, the plural form of *'kruptos'*, a word frequently used by our Lord in the Gospel accounts, and twice by the apostle Paul.[3] It is used in Luke 8:17, where Jesus said, "for nothing is hidden that will not be revealed." Paul uses it in the same sense when writing about "the day when God will judge the secrets of men"[4] and also when he writes about the unbeliever coming into the assembly of God, being convicted and judged by all, "and thus the secrets of his heart are revealed. So he will fall down on his face and worship God, declaring that God is amongst you indeed."[5]

Mankind has his secret things—all to be brought to light in due time. God too has His secret things, which could not be known until He chose to reveal them.

The New Testament is not only the answer to the Old—though it is that, but it is far more! It is the *unfolding* of the secret things which God had purposed in His heart before the worlds were made or the ages began to run their course.

Before beginning our study of the secret things now made known in the New Testament, it will be helpful to briefly notice the *'revealed things'* of the former revelation.

---

[2] The primary Greek translation of the Old Testament.   [3] The passages where it occurs, in its various forms, are: Matt. 6:4,6,18; 13:35; Luke 8:17; 11:33; John 7:4,10; 18:20; 19:38; Rom. 2:16; 1 Cor. 14:25; and Eph. 5:12.   [4] Rom. 2:16   [5] 1 Cor. 14:25

THE REVEALED THINGS

Revelation came to fallen mankind. The first great promise was made, with Adam as witness, in the curse pronounced upon the serpent: the Offspring of the woman will bruise his head. This is evidently "the promise of the life which is in Christ Jesus", which was "promised before time began." [6]

To Abraham it was declared, that as the dust of the earth, the sand of the sea, and the stars of the heaven, so would his offspring be. He was separated from the rest of the nations to be the guardian of the promise. "All the nations of the earth will be blessed by your offspring." [7]

Further divine revelation was delivered through Moses regarding the Prophet to be raised up to whom all were to obey or they would perish. Moses also outlined the future history of the nation. Settled in the land of Canaan by divine power, they would nevertheless be driven away from it because of their disobedience, and end up scattered amongst the Gentiles, to be disgraced and ostracized wherever they wandered. Upon their repentance, they would be reestablished in the land, and made the head of the nations, no longer the tail.

Later prophets elaborated on this, connecting the promised restoration with the *Messiah,* now revealed as the virgin's Son, the One "whose goings out are from of old, from ancient times," [8] yet who was to suffer and die at the hands of men, to endure being forsaken by God, to make reconciliation for sinfulness, but, to prolong His days in resurrection and to be made the King of Israel, sitting on David's throne.

Through Him, the believing part of the nation would be settled in their land, and the apostate portion destroyed. He will judge amongst the nations, rooting out the wicked from the earth and bringing all the righteous into subjection to Israel.

These were the *'revealed things'* and they occur on the earth. They have to do with an earthly people, not a heavenly one. "The heavens are the LORD's heavens, but he has given the

---

[6] 2 Tim. 1:1,9; Tit. 1:2   [7] Gen. 22:18   [8] Mic. 5:2

earth to the children of men." [9] This is the consistent testimony of the prophets in the Old Testament scriptures.

But no matter how hard one looks, there is no hint of the church—the body of Christ—in the things revealed by the prophets. The long age of Christendom is passed over in silence. The Old Testament does not address these things. It was also not made known there that man would be in heaven. The taking up of Enoch and Elijah were strange phenomena to the Jew, of which their Scriptures offered no explanation. All these were amongst 'the secret things' which would not be revealed until the coming of the Just One, to be followed by His rejection and ascension as Man to heaven.

Thus one looks unsuccessfully for the distinctive truths of the Christian era in the Old Testament. The things revealed there refer to Israel and the nations as such and not to the church of which Christ is the glorified Head in heaven.

The amazing thing is that in Christendom at large, despite the revelation of the mysteries of God given in the last portion of our Bibles, the vast majority are so ignorant of the once secret things, it is almost as if they had never been made known. Take the so-called Apostle's Creed for a conclusive example. It will be found that for almost every one of its statements, the proof-texts could be found in the Law, the Prophets, and the Psalms. "He ascended into heaven," is perhaps the only clause in it which the Old Testament did not make known; yet even that is more than hinted at in Psalm 110, and the last verse of Hosea 5. (It is true, as we have just noticed, that these scriptures did not make it clear that He would be in heaven as Man, but, connecting them with other passages in the writings of the Prophets, it would be logical to conclude that He must be.) In other words, the creed affirms virtually nothing of the mystery doctrines revealed in the New Testament, yet it remains one of the most popular Christian statements of faith.

---

[9] Psa. 115:16

CHAPTER 2

Stewards of the Mysteries of God

*E*VERY devoted Christian believer ought to find the widespread ignorance referred to in the closing paragraph of the previous chapter most troubling. After all, if God has in our day plainly revealed things kept secret from the foundation of the world, it is surely in our best interest and to God's glory to understand and value them.

Isaiah could write the words which the apostle Paul later quotes: "Things which an eye didn't see, and an ear didn't hear, which didn't enter into the heart of man, these God has prepared for those who love him." [1] But the apostle does not stop there, as many Christians do. He immediately adds: "But to us, God revealed them through the Spirit. For the Spirit searches all things, yes, the deep things of God." [2]

Clearly, then, there are precious truths which, even as late as Isaiah's time, were amongst the *'secret things'*, but which have now been added to things which are revealed, and which are for us and for our children. It is to these things Paul refers when he writes at the beginning of 1 Corinthians 4, "so let a man think of us as Christ's servants, and stewards of God's mysteries."

The Greek word *'musterion'* used here—which is anglicized in our English word *'mysteries'*—refers to secret things known only to the initiated. It is not that the things in themselves were mysterious and beyond finite comprehension, or even above the range of ordinary minds. Rather, it was information that would

---

[1] Isa. 64:4 [2] 1 Cor. 2:9,10

never be known at all unless revealed by another. A well-known first century example of this were the Eleusinian Mysteries: annual initiations into the cult of Demeter and Persephone based at Eleusis in ancient Greece. Their mysteries were cultic teachings not known by the broader public, but revealed only to a select group of initiates.

As used in our New Testament, the *'mysteries'* are those truths which in Old Testament days God kept in silence, but which are now the common possession of all believers. They are not special truths for a special class, but every Christian has the privilege of knowing these mysteries. Even more than that, no Christian can properly begin to fulfill the responsibilities flowing from the relationship in which we stand toward God if he or she remains ignorant of these same mysteries.[3]

Christ's ministers are to be stewards of the mysteries of God, not merely preachers of what people so often call *'the simple gospel.'* Out of their treasure they are to bring forth things new and old, if instructed in the mysteries of the kingdom of heaven.[4] It is not as if these things are of an obscure or impractical nature—no, quite the opposite! They are the very lines of truth which, above all others, tend to form the character and guide the ways of the Christian. If we accept the preferred reading of 1 Corinthians 2:1, it is to these very things that the apostle referred when he wrote, "When I came to you, brothers, I didn't come with excellence of speech or of wisdom, proclaiming to you the mystery of God." And yet he immediately adds in the next verse, "For I determined not to know anything amongst you except Jesus Christ and him crucified." But "Jesus Christ, and Him crucified" will never be truly known, in the way the apostle intends, if we are content to go on in ignorance of the mysteries.

---

[3] The word *'musterion'* is found twenty-seven times in the Textus Receptus manuscripts of the New Testament: Matt. 13:11; Mark 4:11; Luke 8:10; Rom. 11:25; 16:25; 1 Cor. 2:7; 4:1; 13:2; 14:2; 15:51; Eph. 1:9; 3:3,4,9; 5:32; 6:19; Col. 1:26,27 (twice); 2:2; 4:3; 2 Thess. 2:7; 1 Tim. 3:9,16; Rev. 1:20; 10:7; 17:5,7. (And 1 Cor. 2:1, where *'marturion'* seems to be a copyist's error for *'musterion'*.)
[4] See Matt. 13:52.

Rome, we know, has attempted to convince the church that its legendary traditions and sacramental observances are the mysteries, in a way not much different than the pagan cults, which had their inner secrets for the special few. But the Christian mysteries are for every child of God in this age of grace. Nor are they of an occult or metaphysical nature, appealing only to mystics or elite scholars. No, they are simple truths of tremendous importance, some of which, at least, have been utterly ignored by the vast majority of theologians, ancient and modern, and this to their shame and loss.

It has often been remarked that every teaching which the apostles start with an expression such as, *'I don't desire you to be ignorant, brothers, of this mystery,'* ends up being a doctrine which, after twenty centuries of Christianity, the bulk of professing believers know little or nothing about. It will only be necessary to refer to the relevant New Testament passages to see how true this observation is.

In Romans Paul writes, "I don't desire you to be ignorant, brothers, of this mystery, so that you won't be wise in your own conceits, that a partial hardening has happened to Israel, until the fullness of the Gentiles has come in, and so all Israel will be saved. Even as it is written, 'There will come out of Zion the Deliverer, and he will turn away ungodliness from Jacob.'" [5] Now, how often does the audience hear any reference to *'the fullness of the Gentiles'* or the *'salvation of Israel as a nation'* from the pulpit? Not often. And as a result, the Gentiles are wise in their own conceits, boasting of the imminent conversion of the world, and the transference of Jewish promises to the church of God.

Again, this time writing of the rapture of the saints at the return of our Lord, the same apostle says: "we don't want you to be ignorant, brothers, concerning those who have fallen asleep, so that you don't grieve like the rest, who have no hope," [6] and he proceeds to comfort them with teaching about the raising of the dead, and the simultaneous catching up of the living at the

Lord's return, which—it is not too much to say—not one Christian in ten knows much about.

Peter writes of the second coming of the Lord Jesus, and says: "But don't forget this one thing, beloved, that one day is with the Lord as a thousand years, and a thousand years as one day," [7] and with this he pairs solemn and important truth as to the *'day of the Lord'* and the *'day of God'*—and probably not a saint in a hundred knows the difference between the two terms.

What do Christians have to say to this? What can thousands say for failing to value and take hold of mysteries of such tremendous importance? Failing to take hold of these things, the church has lost the sense of her pilgrim character—confusing teaching relating to Israel and the nations, with divine instruction regarding the body of Christ. The heavenly calling has been lost sight of, and practically given up, for an earthly one.

Unquestionably, the burden of blame rests upon the guides who, professing to be Christ's ministers, are anything but stewards of the mysteries of God. Many are undeniably stewards of science, of philosophy, of politics, of economics, of literature, of historic lore, and of religious notions. But it is quite another thing to be dispensers of the now-revealed secret things which for past ages were hidden in God.

But not all the blame rests upon the leaders of religious thought, as they are called. In Jeremiah's day he could declare, "The prophets prophesy falsely, and the priests rule by their own authority; and my people love to have it so," therefore he solemnly asks, "What will you do in the end of it?" [8] The people love to have it so! This is highly significant. Heretical teachers could not survive for one day if the people did not wish for their ministry. And preachers of Old Testament truths (which they offer in place of New Testament mysteries) would not find it so easy to go on confusing the people of God if there was a real exercise of conscience amongst those who are otherwise content to be labelled *'the laity,'* and who rarely read their

---

[7] 2 Pet. 3:8   [8] Jer. 5:31

Bibles for themselves, and seldom attempt to rightly divide the word of truth. [9]

Do not misunderstand. The study and teaching of the Old Testament is not to be minimized or ignored! It is of the utmost importance that our souls be established in all that is revealed there, in order that we may mature towards the perfection of the full Christian revelation.

Kindergarten and primary school classes are fundamentally important, but it is not a sound principle of education to keep people going over the alphabet when their age and intelligence suggests university level comprehension is possible, if properly instructed. The Old Testament is "the teaching of the first principles of Christ," [10] which the apostle exhorts us to leave, that we may go on to full growth—that is, Christianity. It is not that he would have us forget the beginning, any more than the university student forgets the instruction of the primary school. The student leaves it and moves on, but continues to carry with them the knowledge they received there.

In the following chapter, we plan then to leave the revealed things of the past dispensation, and go on to contemplate the mysteries of God which He has now made known for our spiritual growth and blessing.

---

[9]See 2 Tim. 2:15.   [10]Heb. 6:1

CHAPTER 3

The Mystery of the Kingdom of Heaven

"To you, it is given" said the Lord, speaking to His disciples, "to know the mysteries of the Kingdom of Heaven." [1]

Heaven's rule over earth was no new teaching. For centuries, the prophets had preached about it, pointing ahead to a coming day when everyone would witness it. And this was not merely some measure of spiritual influence exercised by the Lord from heaven, but a true earthly kingdom, destroying and superseding all other human governments, and characterized by the universal spread of spiritual teaching and divine authority. This much is made very plain in the Old Testament scriptures.

This promised kingdom is to be administered through the elect remnant of Israel; the Gentiles being blessed, as their subjects. To attempt to list the Bible passages which teach these prophetic truths, would be to quote the major part of the Psalms and the Prophets.

Daniel, perhaps more plainly than any other, unfolds the glories of that coming reign of righteousness. Through a supernatural vision, Babylon's proud king was allowed to view a stone that fell from heaven, shattering the image of Gentile dominion, and becoming a great mountain that filled the whole earth. [2] This is clearly a far different thing than Christianity, for Gentile dominion is not yet destroyed, nor is there any

---

[1] Matt. 13:11   [2] See Dan. 2.

likelihood that it will be accomplished by the spread of the gospel and extending the boundaries of Christendom.

And yet, clearly, there is a spiritual kingdom of heaven throughout the world at the present time—but with the King Himself absent in the heavens. This is what the greater part of Matthew's Gospel deals with. In fact, without understanding this, it is quite impossible to truly comprehend that first Gospel account.

THE KINGDOM IN MATTHEW'S GOSPEL

Glancing briefly at this interesting book, we find in chapter one the genealogy of the promised King—Son of David, Son of Abraham. In chapter two, the Gentiles (Magi from the east) pay Him honour—foreshadowing the day when all nations will acknowledge His benevolent yet righteous rule.   John the Baptist comes before us in chapter three with the startling cry, "the Kingdom of Heaven is at hand!" [3] He is no doubt referring to Daniel's visions. The reign of heaven over the earth had, by John's time, come so close that the King could now be offered to Israel. If they received Him, He was there in person to establish His kingdom. In the latter part of the chapter, Christ is baptized in the Jordan river, and in doing so, is identifying Himself with the remnant who admit their unfitness for the kingdom John is proclaiming.

The fourth chapter opens with Satan's offer of the kingdom apart from the cross, only to be rebuked by the rightful Ruler, who, leaving the wilderness, goes about preaching and healing, saying, "Repent! For the Kingdom of Heaven is at hand," [4] thus authenticating the message of John.

In chapters five to seven, He outlines the governing principles that will be enacted when that kingdom is fully set up. Yet, in closing, He explains that not all who say "Lord, Lord," will enjoy the blessings of that reign—only those who receive His words, and do them.

---

[3] Matt. 3:2   [4] Matt. 4:17

From this point on, He experiences ever-increasing rejection, as chapters eight to eleven make clear to us. Near the end of that passage, He denounces the cities that had seen His mighty works; and then, turning from the thought of the kingdom which they had rejected, He extends the call of the gospel to weary souls everywhere. "Come to me, all you who labour and are heavily burdened, and I will give you rest."[5] If Israel will not acknowledge Him as King, He remains the Saviour of sinners, and the giver of rest to the burdened.

In chapter twelve, the leaders of the nation commit the unpardonable sin for which they shall never be forgiven, in this age or that to come. The kingdom offer is therefore withdrawn for the present, because the King is definitely and finally rejected by the unbelieving masses.

It is at this point in time that He begins to make known the mysteries of Heaven's reign. Up until now He has been going over what the prophets had predicted. They had also told of the ultimate reception of the King, when Israel shall be born again, and made willing to receive Him in the day of His power. The interval between the cutting off of Messiah[6] and His return in glory to take the kingdom, was vaguely described as a time of sorrow for Israel, but what form the reign of Heaven would take during that undefined period had not been revealed. It is this which the Lord now makes known to His disciples, who, refusing to align themselves with the judgment of the nation, had believed in Him. Heaven's reign would proceed, even though the kingdom, as such, had been refused. The King was going up to the heavens, but He would rule from there, and the administration of the kingdom would be committed to the hands of men. This is the key to the seven parables of Matthew's chapter thirteen.

---

[5] Matt. 11:28   [6] See Dan. 9:26.

THE FOUR SOILS

The first parable is not, properly speaking, a likeness of the kingdom at all. It gives, rather, the means by which that kingdom, in its spiritual aspect, was formed. Rejected as Messiah, the Lord went about as a farmer, planting the word. Amongst those who profess to receive that word, there are various classes (Matthew 13:3–8, 18–23). Road-side hearers listen, but go no further. Rocky-ground hearers profess to receive the word, but there is no root, as tribulation and persecution for the truth's sake soon uncover. Those who receive the word amongst thorns allow not only the legitimate things of life, but also covetousness and worldly anxieties, to choke it, so that they become unfruitful. The good-soil hearers are those who truly receive the word and understand it, thus producing fruit.

It is "the word of the kingdom." All who claim to receive it constitute the kingdom of the heavens in its present spiritual form. In other words, the term *the kingdom of heaven,'* as used in Matthew—and in Matthew only—is practically synonymous with *'Christendom'*, which simply means Christ's kingdom. It is that realm on earth where Christ's authority is openly acknowledged, and where His word is honoured, at least in an outward way.

This chapter is being written in the year 1908;[7] but that is not the method of dating the Jews, the Muslims, or the pagans use. The Jews calculate dates from the creation of the world, according to Hebrew traditions; the Muslims, from the hegira[8] of Mohammed; while each of the various heathen nations has special events from which to count, such as the Japanese Era, for instance. But in Christendom, people acknowledge the birth of One who, though rejected, is the true and rightful Sovereign of the universe. So they write *'in the year of our Lord.'*[9] By doing so, they affirm His authority, however much their lives may deny it in practice.

---

[7] The date the author originally wrote.   [8] The time of the escape of the Islamic Prophet from Mecca to Medina to avoid assassination.   [9] Or *'anno Domini'*, the equivalent phrase in Latin; 'A.D.' for short.

Now, within this wider realm of Christendom is found a narrower one, consisting only of those who have truly received the word of the kingdom into their hearts. These are the true citizens of Matthew 18:3, who have "become as little children," and thus "enter into the Kingdom of Heaven." The rest, while within the influence or administration of the kingdom, have never really entered it, in as much as it is a spiritual thing, and requires new birth before one can *'see'* it.[10] In the present age, this re-born company has, by the baptism of the Spirit, been formed into the church, the body of Christ, as we shall see more clearly when we consider the mystery of the one body, in a subsequent chapter. Here, it is only necessary to grasp the difference between being in the kingdom in an outward aspect and being the true children of the kingdom. This is what the next parable emphasizes—the one about the wheat and the weeds.

THE WHEAT AND THE WEEDS

In Matthew 13:24–30, our Lord uses another parable to explain what the Kingdom is like. He does not leave us to work out what it means, however. In verses 37 to 43, He graciously takes time to explain it Himself, answering the request of His disciples: "Explain to us the parable of the darnel weeds of the field."[11]

The Sower of the good seed, He explains, is the Son of man. It was Himself coming with grace into a world in which there was nothing for God, to sow the incorruptible seed—the word of life— that there subsequently might be a harvest to His glory.

"The field is the world."[12] This is of great importance. By making the field represent the church, many Bible students have gone astray. The world, not the church, is the scene where the seed is sown. Here, in the world, the darnel weeds[13] are planted by Satan and his helpers. It is "the enemy who sowed them." Satan has been busy sowing (in the same place where the

---

[10]See John 3:3.   [11]Matt. 13:36   [12]Matt. 13:38   [13]Darnel is a weed grass (probably bearded darnel) that looks very much like wheat until it is mature, when the difference becomes very apparent.

good seed has been scattered) the evil seed of false and unholy teaching which deceives those who receive it. Those who accept the false doctrines, the "destructive heresies"[14] referred to by the apostle Peter, are the children of the devil. They have a worldly reputation of being alive, but are spiritually dead;[15] calling themselves Christians, they are actually the enemies of the cross of Christ. But they are not to be rooted out, as the Roman Crusades once sought to do, in case the good be rooted out with the evil. But both are to grow together until the harvest at the end of the age. For—please take note—it is not the end of the world, but "at the end of this age"[16] that is being designated as the harvest time.

When the age finishes, the weeds will be gathered into bundles and thrown into a furnace of fire. The righteous will then shine as brightly as the sun in the kingdom of their Father. All this will be explained further in other portions as we go on.

So, having explained for us the first two parables, our Lord proceeds to share other ones, which, with the key already given, can be understood when we compare one portion of scripture with another.

THE MUSTARD SEED

Continuing through Matthew 13, the parable of the mustard seed is given in verses 31 and 32. The kingdom of the heavens is described as like a grain of mustard seed, which, having been planted in a field, developed into a great tree. So great, that the birds of the air come and lodge in its branches. This portrays the outward aspect of the kingdom. It has become a great thing in the earth.

A tree is often used as the symbol of worldly power and glory. In the Old Testament, Nebuchadnezzar is given a dream about a great tree, representing him and his kingdom. "It is you, O king, that have grown and become strong; for your greatness has grown, and reaches to the sky, and your dominion to the end of the earth."[17] The kingdom, or empire, of Assyria is

---

[14] 2 Pet. 2:1   [15] See Rev. 3:1.   [16] Matt. 13:40   [17] Dan. 4:22

portrayed in a similar fashion in Ezekiel 31:3–7: a cedar of high stature, exalted above all the trees of the field, with the birds of the sky nesting in its boughs. The rebellious house of Judah is also described in nearly the same way in Ezekiel 17.

Outwardly, the kingdom of the heavens was to assume an aspect of grandeur upon earth. This has been fulfilled in the history of Christendom. Without question, the 'church' is a power to be reckoned with in the world today, and has been since the days of Constantine.[18] But who are the birds of the air that lodge in the branches of the mustard tree? Recall that in the first parable (the four soils) they were declared to be the powers of Satan. They no doubt mean the same here. (In Revelation 18:2, fallen Babylon is to be the habitation of demons, and the prison of every unclean and hateful bird.)   These are evil workers and false teachers who continue to operate in the professing church. Another parable connects very closely with this, in the verse that follows—that of the leaven.

THE LEAVEN

Matthew 13:33 reads: "He spoke another parable to them. 'The Kingdom of Heaven is like yeast, which a woman took, and hid in three measures of meal, until it was all leavened.'" This is a simple parable to comprehend, since a leavening agent, such as yeast, is commonly added to dough to make it ferment and rise.

However, few portions of the word of God have been more misunderstood than this parable.   It is often interpreted as illustrating the triumph of the gospel, which, like leaven, is supposed to be permeating the world, and will continue to do so until all mankind are saved. If this is its meaning, it is directly opposed to the universal testimony of Scripture elsewhere. Nowhere is it hinted at that the entire world will eventually be converted through the preaching of the gospel as we now know it. The Lord Jesus declared the very opposite; that at His return,

---

[18]Constantine the Great was 57th Emperor of the Roman Empire until his death in 337 A.D., and the first Roman emperor to convert to Christianity. He commissioned the building of the Church of the Holy Sepulchre in Jerusalem.

He will find the evil days of Noah and of Lot reproduced.[19] Neither is leaven, in Scripture, ever a symbol of anything good; nor meal (flour or ground grain) used to represent unregenerate mankind.

Leaven, throughout the Bible, is evil and false. It was to be carefully kept out of the Levitical offerings, which provided a picture of the sinlessness of the Lord Jesus Christ. In the offering of thanksgiving[20] and the loaves at Pentecost[21] leaven was permitted because it pictured the fallen nature of those redeemed by grace. In the New Testament, the Lord warns against the *'leaven of the Pharisees'*, which is hypocrisy;[22] the *'leaven of the Sadducees'*, which is false teaching;[23] and the *'leaven of Herod'*, which is a combining of the world's politics with religion.[24]   Paul writes of "the yeast of malice and wickedness" and contrasts with it "the unleavened bread of sincerity and truth."[25] Therefore, if leaven in the parable of Matthew 13 represents something good and pleasing to God, it would be in direct opposition to the only use made of it elsewhere by the Lord Himself, and by all the rest of Scripture.

On the other hand, three measures of meal, instead of picturing unregenerate mankind—full of sin and wickedness —always speaks, in Scripture typology, of that which is good and useful for spiritual enrichment. It was "three seahs of fine meal"[26] which Sarah quickly prepared, at Abraham's request, to feed to the *'three men'* who came to him in the plains of Mamre. The meat or meal-offering specified in Leviticus 2, showcasing the undefiled and undefilable humanity of the Lord Jesus, was made of meal from which all leaven had been rigidly excluded.

Allowing scripture to explain scripture, it is apparent that the parable of the leaven teaches the very opposite to what it is commonly understood to mean. The meal is the food of the people of God, "that good thing which was committed to you"[27] by the Lord and His apostles. But a mysterious woman has risen up who secretly introduces evil into that which should have

---

[19] See Matt. 24:37 and Luke 17:28–29, for example.   [20] See Lev. 7:12.   [21] See Lev. 23:17.   [22] See Luke 12:1.   [23] See Matt. 16:12.   [24] See Mark 8:14.   [25] 1 Cor. 5:8   [26] Gen. 18:6   [27] 2 Tim. 1:14

remained unleavened, or undefiled. Is it too much to say that this woman is identified for us, in the letter Christ Jesus dictates to the assembly in Thyatira, as "your woman, Jezebel"[28]; and in the vision given to John, as "Babylon the Great?"[29] It is the false church, the great Anti-Church of the Christian centuries, which has assumed the place of teacher instead of learner, and has literally tampered with every precious truth of Scripture. We will discover more of this when we come to consider the *mystery of lawlessness* in a future chapter.

The four parables we have been looking at were spoken in the open air, by the seaside. They show the beginning and the growth of Christendom in both its outward aspect and its true character.

Sending the crowds away, and going into the house, the Lord gave deeper insight to His own disciples, teaching them additional kingdom truths with three more analogies. These too, have often been quite misunderstood. Let's take a moment to briefly notice their teaching.

THE HIDDEN TREASURE

First, He tells of a treasure hid in a field. "Again, the Kingdom of Heaven is like treasure hidden in the field, which a man found, and hid. In his joy, he goes and sells all that he has, and buys that field."[30] Remembering that "the field is the world" we ask, *what is the hidden treasure?*

All throughout the Old Testament, Israel is pictured as a treasure. They formed Jehovah's *'peculiar treasure'*, or *'special possession.'* Messiah came from glory to them, but the time had not yet arrived for His acceptance. So He *'hid'* it, and then went to the cross to pay the purchase price for the whole world[31]— the field, not merely the treasure. That special treasure remains hidden for now, but it will soon be brought out from its hiding place, and He will acknowledge it as His own. "They shall be

---

[28]Rev. 2:20   [29]Rev. 17:5   [30]Matt. 13:44   [31]See 1 John 2:2.

Mine, says the Lord of hosts, in that day when I make up My peculiar treasure." [32]

So it is the earthly aspect of the kingdom which will hopefully be made clearer as we proceed. The parable that follows has some striking differences, though in some ways it is similar.

THE PEARL OF GREAT PRICE

"Again, the Kingdom of Heaven is like a man who is a merchant seeking fine pearls, who having found one pearl of great price, he went and sold all that he had, and bought it." [33]

The businessman seeking fine pearls illustrates the value of the true kingdom in God's own eyes. For He, not the sinner, is the merchant. If salvation was a pearl of great price, no one could ever buy it! For all those unsaved are bankrupt and unprofitable in their efforts. Neither is there any that seek after God.

But He who was rich, became poor on our behalf, leaving the glory that He had with the Father before the earth even existed, and came into this scene to seek a fine pearl to adorn His crown forever. He did discover one pearl, and one of great value! This is the heavenly aspect of the kingdom—the church for which He gave Himself. At Calvary's cross He paid the full price of its purchase, and now no one can dispute His ownership of that church which He has purchased with His own blood. "Christ also loved the assembly, and gave himself up for it." [34]

None of the failure and apostasy of Christendom can alter the value, or touch the purity, of this pearl so greatly prized. Amid all the corruptions of the centuries, it remains perfect and lovely in His eyes. Soon it will be removed from its surroundings of evil and filthiness, and be placed in its proper setting, to be the chief ornament of His crown throughout eternal ages.

---

[32] Mal. 3:17—as a literal translation.   [33] Matt. 13:45–46   [34] Eph. 5:25

THE DRAGNET

The story of the dragnet closes the series. Cast into the sea and dragged along, the net gathers fish of every kind, good and bad. When it is full, the good are collected into containers and the bad are thrown away. The Lord Himself explains: "So will it be in the end of the world. The angels will come and separate the wicked from amongst the righteous, and will cast them into the furnace of fire. There will be the weeping and the gnashing of teeth." [35]

The word commonly translated 'world' in that verse is more accurately translated 'age', similar to the usage in Matthew 12:32. At the end of the age, then, instead of a converted world, we find good and bad being separated by angelic agents. The good are the true children of the kingdom, and are saved eternally. The bad are false professors, caught up in the Christian net, but who have not really received the word of the kingdom in their hearts. Their end is judgment.

Solemnly, the Lord asks, "Have you understood all these things?" [36] They reply that they do, though it is evident from their future interactions that they had only just begun to comprehend the deep truths He had set before them. He adds, "Therefore every scribe who has been made a disciple in the Kingdom of Heaven is like a man who is a householder, who brings out of his treasure new and old things." [37]

The mystery of the seven golden lampstands in Revelation chapters 2 and 3, coincides in a significant way with these seven parables. There we find the seven lampstands symbolize seven local assemblies. Prophetically, they outline seven distinct stages of the professing body, from the apostolic times to the Lord's return. We may compare the parable of the sower, with Ephesus; the wheat and weeds, with Smyrna; the mustard tree, with Pergamos; the leaven, with Thyatira; the treasure, with Sardis; the pearl, with Philadelphia; and the dragnet, with Laodicea. While the focus is often different, the careful student will note that the moral order is practically the same, though of

---

[35] Matt. 13:49–50   [36] Matt. 13:51   [37] Matt. 13:51–52

course, viewed from the standpoint of the assembly rather than the kingdom.   Israel is not brought in, as having no part, nationally, in God's present work.

A few other scriptures require our attention to complete our brief survey of the Master's teaching relating to the reign of the heavens.

In Matthew 16:18, the Lord addresses Peter and we get the first hint of the church—a subject which we will study in coming chapters. To Peter, the Lord adds, "I will give to you the keys of the Kingdom of Heaven, and whatever you bind on earth will have been bound in heaven; and whatever you release on earth will have been released in heaven." Peter, then, is to open the door into the kingdom. It is not into heaven, as some foolishly imagine, nor even into the church that He intends, but into the sphere of Christian discipleship and profession, where the authority of the Lord is acknowledged.   On the day of Pentecost we find Peter using the keys, and admitting the Jews. In the house of Cornelius, he then opens the door to the Gentiles. Since that day, what multitudes have pressed in!

But no one really enters that kingdom, in its true spiritual sense, except those who "turn, and become as little children." [38] Within the borders of the United States you can find people of all nationalities. None are citizens, except those who are born there, or who have renounced their allegiance to every other government. Only they 'enter' the American nation.

The kingdom is the sphere of rule.   So in the latter part of Matthew 18, we have governmental forgiveness illustrated, and afterwards revoked. The question of eternal forgiveness before God, necessary to prepare a soul for heaven, is not what is being discussed here.   A king is settling with those who owe him. Someone is found owing an extremely large sum of money, 'ten thousand talents,' which is about 300 metric tons of silver (equivalent to about 60 million denarii, where one denarius was typical of one day's wages for agricultural labor).

---

[38] Matt. 18:3

Hearing the command that he, his family and all that he had are to be sold, he pleads for mercy. His lord, moved with compassion, forgives the debt. Afterwards, the forgiven man finds another servant who owes him a relatively small amount—100 denarii, which was about one sixtieth of a talent, or about 500 grams (1.1 pounds) of silver. Though the man pleads for pity, none is shown, and he is cast into the debtors' prison. The lord hears of this, and withdraws his mercy.

This is not a question of judgment after death. It is simply the principle upon which forgiveness is granted to those who sin after becoming subjects of the kingdom. "Forgive us our debts, as we also forgive our debtors."[39] The servant who fails to forgive will forfeit his Lord's pardon in His discipline or government on earth, if he does not extend the same grace to his fellow servants. All those who have a part in the kingdom are subjects of grace; but our heavenly Father, "without respect of persons judges according to each man's work"[40] in this life, disciplining and chastening us as His wisdom deems it to be necessary. It is a matter concerning fellowship with God, not our relationship to God. Therefore it ought to motivate me to genuinely forgive my brother's misdeeds, that I may be forgiven myself, and not experience the torment that accompanies an unforgiving spirit.[41]

In the next chapter, Matthew 19, our Lord presents the ideal subject of heaven's reign. "Allow the little children, and don't forbid them to come to me; for the Kingdom of Heaven belongs to ones like these."[42]

The believing parent is encouraged to bring their little ones to the Lord before they end up wandering out into the paths of this world's sin and folly. It is His intention that they grow up in the gracious shelter of the reign of heaven, and that we "nurture them in the discipline and instruction of the Lord."[43] Receiving the word of God in simple faith, they are the models of what every other member of the kingdom should be.

---

[39]Matt. 6:12   [40]1 Pet. 1:17   [41]See Matt. 18:35.   [42]Matt. 19:14   [43]Eph. 6:4

The day when this kingdom is fully displayed will be earth's glorious regeneration, an event the whole creation is waiting for as it groans and struggles in pain because of Adam's fall and its bitter consequences. The Lord refers to this day as he says, "Most certainly I tell you that you who have followed me, in the regeneration when the Son of Man will sit on the throne of his glory, you also will sit on twelve thrones, judging the twelve tribes of Israel."[44] It is to His twelve disciples that He says this—Matthias, presumably, occupying the forfeited place of the traitor Judas Iscariot. (Paul's apostleship was of a different kind, as we shall see when we consider his special mission in connection with the great mystery of Christ and the Church.)

But if this will be the future glory of those who followed the Messiah in His rejection on earth, they become the patterns for all those who will ultimately share in His glory. So another parable of the kingdom immediately follows in Matthew 20:1–16. A master of a house hires laborers to work in his vineyard, and though they work for different lengths of time, they all receive the same wage when the day is over. It is a faithful response to the Master's call that receives reward in the time when service is ended. It will be proved that *'many are called, but few are chosen.'* Everyone is chosen who heeds the call, come when it may: so no one has righteous grounds for complaint.

The mother of James and John then comes to Jesus wanting positions for her sons of power and authority in kingdom. She learns that rejection and death—the terrible baptism of judgment—is in store for the Lord before His day of glory. An undefined period during which His servants will be similarly treated by the world is hinted at, though no clue is given as to its how long it will last.

Christ rules out all thought of a physical kingdom at the present time by warning His disciples that they are not to pattern themselves after the power-hungry rulers of the earthly nations, but are to find their joy in servant-hearted ministry. Sadly, this teaching is so ignored, the words might as well have

---

[44]Matt. 19:28

never been spoken! Christendom today has an abundance of both spiritual and political leaders looking for ways to exercise their authority—and is not bowed with shame, but quite proud of its departure from the Master's command!

In Matthew 21, the King rides triumphantly into Jerusalem, in fulfillment of the prophecy in Zechariah 9:9, while the babes and infants praise, as predicted in Psalm 8:2. But the Lord is careful to express the fact that He is to be put to death and cast out of the vineyard.[45] The kingdom is not to be set up yet.

This, however, will not stop the gospel invitation from being issued. So, in Matthew 22, He gives another analogy of the kingdom of Heaven, showing how, as the King prepares to arrive, a great crowd will be gathered together—from both the Jews and the Gentiles—for the gospel feast. But He warns that those who try to enjoy the feast without having dropped the rags of their own righteousness for the wedding clothing of His providing will not be permitted to stay.

Then He pronounces, in Matthew 23, woes[46] upon those who had rejected His testimony. He concludes with His passionate expression of grief over Jerusalem, and declares that, as a consequence of its continual rejection of the many messengers sent by God, "you will not see me from now on, until you say, 'Blessed is he who comes in the name of the Lord!'"[47]

In His great prophecy on the Mount of Olives (Matthew 24), He explains the sorrows and tribulations through which Israel must pass before they will see the Son of Man returning in power and glory to establish the kingdom prophesied in the Old Testament scriptures. It is because of this rejection of the King —when He came in humility and grace—that they must pass through the time of Jacob's trouble prophesied in Jeremiah 31 before He returns in majesty and judgment.

---

[45]See Matt. 21:33–40. [46]Expressions of great sorrow or distress. [47]Matt. 23:39

Meanwhile, the kingdom of Heaven is likened to ten virgins going out to meet the bridegroom. This is the professing Christians of the present age looking forward to the day of Christ's return. But there are as many foolish as there are wise—true and false are all mixed up together. It is the midnight cry that puts each in their true place. All have been sleeping until aroused by the message, "Behold! The bridegroom is coming! Come out to meet him!"[48] Awakened, some are startled to find their lamp of profession dying out. Others are ready to go in with Him to the marriage. For those lacking oil, it is too late to buy some. When they come back looking to gain entrance, their request is denied.

The next parable in Matthew 25:14–30 is not about the kingdom. Though some Bible translations state it to be, it needs to be remembered that the words printed in italics are not found in the original manuscripts. Instead, the parable pictures the service and reward of those who continue in the King's work during His absence.

The judgment to be executed on the Gentile nations, when the Son of Man comes to take the kingdom and to assert His rights, is portrayed in the remaining verses of Matthew 25.

The rest of the book details the Messiah's final rejection, His mock trial, His death on a cross, and His glorious resurrection. Establishing the crucified, yet risen Jesus as the only Sovereign and Lord, His apostles are instructed to disciple the nations in view of His coming again.

And so, in brief, this is the outline of the mysteries of the Kingdom of Heaven. If one remains ignorant of this topic, the present age becomes a puzzle for which there is no solution.

---

[48] Matt. 25:6

CHAPTER 4

The Mystery of the Olive Tree

*P*AUL's letter to the Romans divides naturally into three parts. Chapters 1 to 8 are *doctrinal*, expounding the gospel of the grace of God in its fullness. Chapters 9 to 11 are *dispensational*, having to do with Israel's past, present, and future. Chapters 12 to 16 are *practical*, giving the results that should flow from the knowledge of the other two portions.

We will focus on the second portion for our study. And first, *what is a dispensation?* The question stumps many, including great preachers such as the late esteemed C.H. Spurgeon who said, when criticizing the writings of another, "Sufficiently taken up with ...dispensational truth, whatever that may mean." Many others are just as as confused when the term is used, though perhaps not so willing to admit it. And yet it is a very scriptural term. *'Dispensation'* is the Greek word *'oikonomia'*, and literally means the *stewardship*, or *administration*, of a household. It is used with this meaning three times in Luke 16:2–4. It occurs four times in our English version of the epistles of Paul, and a careful consideration of these instances will help us be clear about its meaning.

Three times Paul speaks of the dispensation (or *stewardship*) entrusted to him (1 Cor. 9:17; Eph. 3:2; Col. 1:25). As the servant of God, he had received instruction concerning the message for the present age, which he shows us clearly was a two-fold one, embracing both the *truth of the gospel*, and the *truth of the church* (or *assembly*).

He also uses the word in Ephesians 1:10 in reference to a coming age, when he states that in the dispensation (or the *administration*) of "the fullness of the times," all things in heaven and on earth are to be headed up in Christ. But they aren't yet. Hebrews 2:8 tells us that: "But now we don't see all things subjected to him, yet."

So we have here at least two different dispensations clearly distinguished: the one entrusted to Paul, and one to come at the fullness of the times. From this, we can begin to flesh out our understanding of the term that causes confusion for so many. Dispensational truth is comprehending the teaching of Scripture relative to the various dispensations, or stewardships, or administrations, in which mankind has been or will be placed. This is what is meant by a *'dispensation'*. It is a particular order, or governing economy, that God establishes for a particular time in history.

Augustine wrote: "Distinguish the ages, and the Scriptures are plain." Where one does not do this, there exists a mass of confusion—not in the Scriptures, but in the mind of the reader.

It should be clear to even casual Bible students that the nature of God's administration and man's stewardship hasn't remained the same throughout history. The order in effect inside the garden of Eden was different from that outside its gates. The order following the great flood was again different from that prior to the flood.

So we've just identified three dispensations. The first is one of *innocence*. Humanity, without the knowledge of evil, was placed in a home full of wonder. That first dispensation was a most happy one, until it was ended by Adam's fall into sin.

The time between leaving Eden to the great flood of Noah's day, was a long stretch of approximately sixteen hundred years, if we accept the popular chronology. It was a period when mankind had no Bible, and no organized government to provide restraint. He had for a guide what men call the *'light of nature'*, coupled with the *'light of conscience'*. But by the end, corruption and violence was so prevalent that God swept away the wicked world with a global deluge of water. That time was first and foremost a stewardship of *conscience*; but the steward failed catastrophically.

A new administration began when human government was established by God, and governing power and authority was committed to Noah.[1] Here a notable example of the importance of dispensational truth can be seen. In the stewardship before the flood, Cain killed his brother, and, since government was not yet entrusted to man, God appointed a sign for the murderer, so that anyone finding him would not kill him.[2] After the flood, the decree was given: "Whoever sheds man's blood, his blood will be shed by man."[3] Dispensationally, both were in their place.

For the heathen world, there has been no advance in the dispensations since the days of Noah, as Romans 2:12 points out. But upon the decline into universal idolatry that soon followed the reestablishment of mankind on the earth, God called out one man, Abram, from beyond the Euphrates river, where his fathers served other gods, and committed to him a new and glorious dispensation: that of the promise of the *'offspring'* or *'seed'*. In the light of this the patriarchs walked, until moral decline caused the bondage in Egypt.

Through Moses, then, another dispensation was introduced: that of the Law, which lasted from the covenant enacted at Mt. Sinai until the rejection of the Son of God—the *'Offspring'*, whose coming had been prophesied for a long time.

This then opened the way for the current stewardship of the gospel of grace and the assembly—given more fully to Paul than to anyone else. This raises a most important question: *what happens to Israel's hope?*

The dispensational portion of the letter to the Romans is the clear and concise answer to the question.

In Romans 9, it is shown that the promises were made to Israel. The Messiah was to come through them, and He was to be their Deliverer and their King. But having rejected Him, are all the

---

[1] See Gen. 9.   [2] See Gen. 4:15.   [3] Gen. 9:6

people of the chosen nation to be cut off? Chapter 10 supplies the answer. At the present time, there remains an election of grace.[4] All who trust in the One whom the nation as a whole rejects, find in Him a Saviour even now. But this involves breaking their ties with the nation as such, and becoming a part of the church, the body of Christ—something we will look at in a later chapter.

So what happens then, to the promises relating to Israel's earthly power and dominion? Are they ever to be fulfilled? And if they are, how do we account for the current condition of the chosen people during the stewardship of grace? This is addressed fully, yet simply, in the teaching related to the mystery of the olive tree in Romans 11.

THE OLIVE TREE

The olive tree is the tree of privilege. Abraham is the root of this tree, for the Lord had said, "I will bless you and...You will be a blessing...All the families of the earth will be blessed through you."[5] The people of Israel therefore, are the natural branches. The Gentiles are represented as branches of a wild olive tree, grafted contrary to nature into a good olive tree. To them, the apostle Paul addresses a solemn admonition and warning: "For I speak to you who are Gentiles. Since then as I am an apostle to Gentiles, I glorify my ministry; if by any means I may provoke to jealousy those who are my flesh, and may save some of them."[6] That is, he delighted to see God's grace going out to the nations. He hoped that this would cause his fellow Israelites to be stirred up in a holy jealousy and a determination to enjoy for themselves the precious grace of God—that had already been offered to them, but was so carelessly rejected.

"For if the rejection of them is the reconciling of the world, what would their acceptance be, but life from the dead?"[7] According to the prophets, the whole world is to be brought into blessing through the blessing of Israel, in the latter day, under Messiah's rule. If, even now (before the prophetic word is

---

[4]See Rom. 11:5.   [5]Gen. 12:1–3   [6]Rom. 9:13,14   [7]Rom. 9:15

fulfilled,) grace has gone out to the nations, while the people of the promise are cut off because of their sin, who can estimate the abundant favor the whole world will experience when the long-promised restoration has at last become a fact?

Instead of cancelling the promises He made to the fathers of the Hebrews, the rejection of the Messiah has caused God to bring hidden purposes to light—formerly unrevealed—of grace for the Gentiles, lasting an age of undisclosed duration, while the covenant people are partially blinded. Paul goes on to explain this, declaring that God has not forgotten His pledge to Israel, but that their current stumbling is the means God is using to bring previously undreamed-of blessing to the nations. Meanwhile, His ancient people are still dear to His heart, though they are disowned for the time being. The Gentiles are like wild olive branches grafted into a good tree, in place of the natural branches, who, because of unbelief, have been lopped off.[8] This is clearly *contrary to nature*.

One hardly knows whether to pity the ignorance or be upset at the audacity of a critic, who confidently stated that Paul evidently knew very little about grafting, to write about the introduction of wild branches into a good tree, instead of the common practice of introducing good branches into wild trees. This arrogant judge of divine things had not noticed that the intelligent and observant apostle specifically states that such a procedure was *'contrary to nature.'* That is, in fact, the main point of Paul's argument.

To the Gentiles whom God has brought into such noticeable favor, he writes: "Don't boast over the branches. But if you boast, it is not you who support the root, but the root supports you. You will say then, 'Branches were broken off, that I might be grafted in.' True; by their unbelief they were broken off, and you stand by your faith. Don't be conceited, but fear; for if God didn't spare the natural branches, neither will he spare you. See then the goodness and severity of God. Towards those who fell, severity; but towards you, goodness, if you continue in his goodness; otherwise you also will be cut off. They also, if they

---

[8] See Rom. 9:16,17.

don't continue in their unbelief, will be grafted in, for God is able to graft them in again. For if you were cut out of that which is by nature a wild olive tree, and were grafted contrary to nature into a good olive tree, how much more will these, which are the natural branches, be grafted into their own olive tree?" [9]

The argument is clear and consistent throughout. Israel is now rejected because of their unbelief. In the meantime, super-abounding mercy flows out to the Gentiles. God is taking out from them a people for His name. [10]   But if the Gentiles abuse His grace, as Israel did before them, they shall be, in their turn, rejected.   However, if the children of the promise are brought to repentance, they will once more be taken up and blessed according to the promises made throughout the writings of the prophets. Therefore, he solemnly asserts, "For I don't desire you to be ignorant, brothers, of this mystery, so that you won't be wise in your own conceits, that a partial hardening has happened to Israel, until the fullness of the Gentiles has come in." [11] There is a limit to the present dispensation of grace. When that is reached, the fullness of the nations will have arrived, and God will again turn His hand to His ancient people. "And so all Israel will be saved. Even as it is written, 'There will come out of Zion the Deliverer, and he will turn away ungodliness from Jacob. This is my covenant with them, when I will take away their sins.'" [12]

Take care to note that it is not the Redeemer acting from heaven (as He does now); rather it is the Deliverer coming out of Zion—appearing the second time at Jerusalem as the Messiah of Israel, when "they will look to me whom they have pierced; and they shall mourn for him, as one mourns for his only son, and will grieve bitterly for him, as one grieves for his firstborn." [13]

This leads to an outburst of praise on the part of the apostle that must stir every heart in touch with the mind of God. [14] With this, the chapter ends. It is a wonderful unfolding of God's ways—of which, sadly, only a few seem to grasp. Not obeying the warning, the Gentiles, as a result, are lifted up with pride;

---

[9]Rom. 11:18–24   [10]See Acts 15:14.   [11]Rom. 11:25   [12]Rom. 11:26,27   [13]Zech. 12:10   [14]See Rom. 11:33–36.

and, instead of humility and the fear of the Lord, are indulging in boasting similar to those in the Laodicean church of Revelation 3, as though the end of the dispensation was far away, instead of being almost here.

Failing to distinguish between the earthly and the heavenly callings, present-day Christendom has become a sad and strange mixture of Judaism, heathenism, and Christianity. Many have lost sight of the church's special portion and blessed hope, [15] and are cherishing Jewish expectations in their place.

The mystery of the olive tree, if understood and taken to heart, would help correct all this, and would be the means of leading the people of God to distinguish clearly between the two callings. Surely, it is every true believer's responsibility to turn away from the worthless speculations of unspiritual or blind guides, and to search the Scriptures themselves to see whether these things are true. After all, we are exhorted to walk worthy of our calling, [16] and we can only do so if we understand what that calling is.

---

[15] See Tit. 2:11–14.   [16] See Eph. 4:1.

CHAPTER 5

The Great Mystery of Christ and the Church

THROUGHOUT the writings of the apostle Paul, he repeatedly refers to a wondrous secret, which he designates in a special way as *'the mystery,'* or *'the great mystery.'* There are other mysteries that he speaks of—as we have seen, and will also notice later—but there is one particular mystery that emerges as his major theme. Much of his ministry focuses on it, and it is clearly the chief jewel in the crown of the truth of Christianity —yet for centuries, it was almost entirely missed.

In fact, until emphasized through the writings, preaching and teaching of a distinguished ex-clergyman, John Nelson Darby (1800–1880), it is scarcely to be found in a single book or sermon throughout a period of sixteen hundred years! If anyone doubts this statement, let them search[1] the remarks of the so-called Church Fathers, both pre- and post-Nicene; the theological treatises of the scholastic divines; Roman Catholic writers of all shades of thought; the literature of the Reformation; the sermons and expositions of the Puritans; and the general theological works of the day. *'The mystery'* will be conspicuous by its absence. There is much written that elevates ordinances to the place of mysteries, similar to heathen rituals—but as for *'the mystery,'* which was so unspeakably precious to the apostle Paul, it is rarely referenced!

That a doctrine so clearly revealed in the Scriptures could have become so utterly lost is only to be explained by the Judaizing of

---

[1] As the original writer, H.A. Ironside, had done extensively.

43

the Christian church, and the resulting focus on earthly things that ignored the heavenly ones.

In seeking to point out the truth of the great mystery, we will examine the passages in which it is mentioned or explained, in the order in which they are found in our English Bibles.

The first passage is: "Now to him who is able to establish you according to my Good News and the preaching of Jesus Christ, according to the revelation of the mystery which has been kept secret through long ages, but now is revealed, and by the Scriptures of the prophets, according to the commandment of the eternal God, is made known for obedience of faith to all the nations; to the only wise God, through Jesus Christ, to whom be the glory forever! Amen." [2]

The mystery is not explained in depth in Romans. We must turn to Ephesians especially for that. But in Romans, Paul refers to what his special line of ministry was without expounding it. He speaks of the unveiling of the mystery which had previously been kept in silence. Now it is made known—not through the Old Testament—but *'through prophetic writings'* (which is a better translation than "the Scriptures of the prophets"; that is, the mystery is made known in the prophetic writings of the apostle himself). Paul was the chosen vessel who alone was given the responsibility to share the mystery "for obedience of faith." Now if the mystery is for those who have faith to obey, it is vastly important that every child of God be instructed as to its true character.

Before passing on, let's review the main point. The mystery formed no part of the divine revelation given during the previous dispensations. If it had, Paul could not honestly have written that it was "kept secret through long ages." Instead, it was part of the Good News he was commissioned to preach far and wide—but he learned it not from the Old Testament scriptures, but by direct revelation from the Lord Jesus Christ in glory.

[2]Rom. 16:25–27 or in some translations, Rom. 14:24–26.

In 1 Corinthians, Paul, after refusing the wisdom of the world, writes: "We speak wisdom, however, amongst those who are full grown, yet a wisdom not of this world nor of the rulers of this world who are coming to nothing. But we speak God's wisdom in a mystery, the wisdom that has been hidden, which God foreordained before the worlds for our glory, which none of the rulers of this world has known. For had they known it, they wouldn't have crucified the Lord of glory." [3]

Here he does not speak clearly of the mystery of *the assembly*, but he implies that some great and previously unrevealed secret was the burden of his ministry to those already established in the gospel; so it evidently includes that which we are now considering. The crucifixion of the Lord of glory made way for the declaration of this great secret, which had never previously been made known. While the Messiah is on the Father's throne, and the people of Israel are rejected because of their refusal of their King, God is displaying the hidden purpose of His heart in the creation of *'a new thing in the earth,'* even the spiritual body of His Son, to share with Him all the glories He is yet to enter into, when the fulfillment of Old Testament prophecy is resumed.

It is to Paul's letters to the Ephesians and the Colossians we must turn for the further unfolding of this mystery. Its full revelation is declared in Ephesians 1: "making known to us the mystery of his will, according to his good pleasure which he purposed in him to an administration of the fullness of the times, to sum up all things in Christ, the things in the heavens and the things on the earth, in him." [4]

This is God's amazing purpose. Jesus has been set aside by mankind, and with every indignity the wickedness of his heart could devise, has been crucified and slain. Because of this, the prophetic clock stopped at Calvary. Not one tick has been heard since. From the moment Jesus bowed His head and yielded up His Spirit to the Father, all the glories of the kingdom spoken of by Old Testament prophets have been held at bay. God has not

---

[3] 1 Cor. 2:6–8   [4] Eph. 1:9,10

altered His plan, but remains committed to the sure and soon fulfillment, when:

> *Jesus shall reign where'er the sun*
> *Doth his successive journeys run,*
> *His kingdom spread from shore to shore,*
> *Till moons shall wax and wane no more.* [5]

But now God has made known that when that time comes, Christ will not enter into His glories alone!   For in the administration of the fullness of the times—the final dispensation of all, when the liberty of grace shall be succeeded by the liberty of the glory—the last Adam shall not be without someone to share His throne and the glories of His kingdom. The church is that bride, as Ephesians 5 shows.   In the Millennium, it will share with Christ His rule and power when He will be enthroned as the Head of all things, the firstborn, or pre-eminent one, of all creation.

How appropriate it is that He who suffered so humbly, should be exalted so gloriously! But how amazing the grace that leads Him to say of His redeemed: "The glory which you have given me, I have given to them." [6] The Lord Jesus Christ richly deserves His honours.   We deserve only eternal judgment and wrath. But He takes out from Jews and Gentiles—who united to crucify Him—a people who will be so near to Him forever, they are called His body and His bride!

This is what Paul further unfolds for us in Ephesians 3. "By revelation [7] the mystery was made known to me, as I wrote before in few words, by which, when you read, you can perceive my understanding in the mystery of Christ, which in other generations was not made known to the children of men, as it has now been revealed to his holy apostles and prophets in the Spirit, that the Gentiles are fellow heirs and fellow members of the body, and fellow partakers of his promise in Christ Jesus

---

[5] From the hymn *'Jesus Shall Reign'* by Isaac Watts.   [6] John 17:22   [7] Notice it was not by the study of the Old Testament.

through the Good News, of which I was made a servant [8] according to the gift of that grace of God which was given me according to the working of his power. To me, the very least of all saints, was this grace given, to preach to the Gentiles the unsearchable riches of Christ, and to make all men see what is the administration of the mystery which for ages has been hidden in God, who created all things through Jesus Christ, to the intent that now through the assembly the manifold wisdom of God might be made known to the principalities and the powers in the heavenly places." [9]

This is the fullest declaration, or unfolding, of this precious and wondrous mystery that we have in all the Bible. It is so plain, that one would think that every spiritual mind would immediately grasp what it refers to. Yet many commentators and expositors are generally happy to make it mean that in the present age, God is extending to the Gentile the same grace He offers the Jew, so that the former, by accepting His offer of grace, becomes a sharer in the kingdom promised to Israel.

But this interpretation loses sight entirely of that which Paul was commissioned to make known. Israel's blessings are earthly, and for a specific period of time. When they experience them, the Gentile world will bow before the Jews, and admit their superior position. Those who have been the tail for so long, will become the head. This is the universal testimony of the prophets.

The mystery, on the other hand, is spiritual, and belongs to heaven. Taking a pause in His revealed agenda, God now makes known his hidden purpose to take out of Jews and Gentiles a people for heaven, who are to be one with Christ for all eternity. They are baptized by the Holy Spirit into one body, [10] and united by the same Spirit to the Head in heaven—thus permanently linked with Himself. Their realm of blessing is heavenly, so during the present time they are pilgrims on earth. When *the administration of the fullness of the times*' has come, all God's promises to Israel will be fulfilled. They will be blessed on earth.

---

[8] The indefinite article *'a'* is superfluous. He was *servant*, or *minister*, in a distinctive sense, of the gospel of the glory and the mystery.

[9] Eph. 3:3–10

[10] See 1 Cor. 12:13.

And the church will be blessed in heaven. Christ will be the centre of a redeemed universe, and His bride will share in all His acquired glories. This is the mystery—glorious, inconceivably amazing, and transcendently wonderful!

It is what the marriage union on earth is supposed to picture. "Wives, be subject to your own husbands, as to the Lord. For the husband is the head of the wife, as Christ also is the head of the assembly, being himself the saviour of the body. But as the assembly is subject to Christ, so let the wives also be to their own husbands in everything. Husbands, love your wives, even as Christ also loved the assembly, and gave himself up for it; that he might sanctify it, having cleansed it by the washing of water with the word, that he might present the assembly to himself gloriously, not having spot or wrinkle or any such thing; but that it should be holy and without defect ...because we are members of his body, of his flesh and bones. 'For this cause a man will leave his father and mother, and will be joined to his wife. The two will become one flesh.' This mystery is great, but I speak concerning Christ and of the assembly." [11]

It is precious to realize that every joyful Christian home, where the husband and wife live together according to knowledge, [12] is a beautiful picture of this mystery—no longer hidden, but now fully revealed.

When we turn to the companion letter to the saints at Colosse, we find the same deep and blessed theme introduced. After the twofold headship of the Lord Jesus has been proclaimed (head of all creation and head of the assembly), [13] and the twofold aspect of reconciliation is unfolded (for the individual right now, and for *'all things'* in the future), [14] we are told of Paul's twofold ministry. [15] Just as in Ephesians, Paul is minister both of the gospel and of the church.

He writes: "Now I rejoice in my sufferings for your sake, and fill up on my part that which is lacking of the afflictions of Christ in my flesh for his body's sake, which is the assembly, of

---

[11] Eph. 5:22–32   [12] See 1 Pet. 3:7.   [13] See Col. 1:15–19.   [14] See Col. 1:20–22.
[15] See Col. 1:23–29.

which I was made a servant according to the stewardship of God which was given me towards you to fulfil[16] the word of God, the mystery which has been hidden for ages and generations. But now it has been revealed to his saints, to whom God was pleased to make known what are the riches of the glory of this mystery amongst the Gentiles, which is Christ in you,[17] the hope of glory. We proclaim him, admonishing every man and teaching every man in all wisdom, that we may present every man perfect in Christ Jesus; for which I also labour, striving according to his working, which works in me mightily."[18]

This, along with the opening verses of Ephesians 2, concludes the testimony relating to this wonderful mystery, so far as the actual use of the word is concerned. But every diligent student must observe, once their eyes are opened to it, that this mystery forms the bulk of the teaching left for our spiritual growth by Paul, the apostle to the nations.

What is important to grasp here is that the mystery is the great truth that completes the word of God. It is the capstone of Scripture teaching, just as the cross is the foundation-stone of the gospel. Christ is now working amongst the Gentiles, while rejected by Israel. This, the Old Testament did not consider. That the nations would be brought, through Israel, to recognize Christ's authority is clearly taught. But that He would be doing a special work amongst them, while the Jews are set aside, was a secret hidden in God. To understand this is to enter into the truth for the present dispensation. Therefore, the Lord's servant Paul ministered with steadfast perseverance so that those already saved might be taught what is of such great importance to all who want to experience, not stunted growth, but full development and maturity in Christ Jesus.

This is why he goes on to say, "For I desire to have you know how greatly I struggle for you, and for those at Laodicea, and for as many as have not seen my face in the flesh; that their hearts may be comforted, they being knit together in love, and gaining all riches of the full assurance of understanding, that they may

---

[16]Or, 'to complete'.   [17]Or, 'amongst you'.   [18]Col. 1:24–29

know the mystery of God, both of the Father and of Christ, in whom all the treasures of wisdom and knowledge are hidden." [19]

The mystery of God is Christ—Christ, the spiritual Head of His spiritual body! As man, He sits on God's throne, as the Head of the church. His members on earth are those redeemed by His blood and baptized by the Holy Spirit into one body. Thus the great secret has two parts: one, relating to the Head; the other, to the body.

It was undreamed of in past ages that Man would sit on the throne of the universe. It was also unthinkable to a Jew that the middle wall of separation should ever be broken down, [20] and the saved of those both inside and outside formed into one new man. But God has made happen what, for anyone but Himself, would have been impossible. May we more fully enter into what is so precious to His great heart of love!

---

[19]Col. 2:1–3   [20]See Eph. 2:14.

CHAPTER 6

The Mystery of Godliness

"Without controversy, the mystery of godliness is great:
God was revealed in the flesh,
justified in the spirit,
seen by angels,
preached amongst the nations,
believed on in the world,
and received up in glory."[1]

THIS is the battle cry of the soldiers of the new dispensation. *The mystery of godliness has been revealed in the flesh!* The God of heaven has appeared on earth, with a human body permanently united to His divine nature, and "we saw his glory, such glory as of the one and only Son of the Father, full of grace and truth."[2] To deny this truth, is to fall away from the faith, and to surrender any right to call yourself a Christian.

In fact, it is by this confession that spirits are to be tried and the claims of teachers to be evaluated. "By this you know the Spirit of God: every spirit who confesses that Jesus Christ has come in the flesh is of God, and every spirit who doesn't confess that Jesus Christ has come in the flesh is not of God, and this is the spirit of the Antichrist, of whom you have heard that it comes. Now it is in the world already."[3]

No truth has been more bitterly denied and no teaching more relentlessly attacked by Satan's dark forces—often disguising themselves as angels of light—than this one. Not only the unbelieving Jews, but heretics of all ages since the cross of

[1] 1 Tim. 3:16   [2] John 1:14   [3] 1 John 4:2,3

Christ, have aimed their poisonous darts at this most precious mystery of godliness. Yet, it lives on today as the cherished ark carried by the people of the Lord through the wilderness of this world, on their pilgrimage from the cross to the glory.

And indeed, it was this very truth that the Ark of the Covenant illustrated. There, the gold represented the divine nature; and the acacia wood—the incorruptible wood of the desert—pictured the human nature of our Lord Jesus Christ. Here was God's throne. Here He could rest—not in a mere creature to be sure, but in His own eternal Son who took on flesh, and accomplished His will perfectly in the scene where He had been so terribly dishonoured.

Though subject to unceasing attack by unbelievers, it is not on imprecise and vague statements of scripture that the believer rests their faith that Jesus is very God and very Man, two natures in one person, inseparable and indissoluble.

OLD TESTAMENT PROPHECY

The Old Testament does speak of this mystery, but in such a way that only *after* Christ had come, could its statements and predictions be clearly understood. The second Psalm subtly portrayed His rejection by the nations and the people of Israel, and then adds in verse seven: "I will tell of the decree: The LORD said to me, 'You are my son. Today I have become your father.'" Jehovah God could not speak to a mere creature like this. Between the Creator and the greatest of His creation, there is an immeasurable distance. No, it is to the Lord Jesus he is speaking; it is the deity of the Son that the Psalm declares.

The prophet Zechariah declares the reality of His manhood, while implying His equality with Jehovah God, when he writes, "'Awake, sword, against my shepherd, and against the man who is close to me,' says the LORD of Armies. 'Strike the shepherd, and the sheep will be scattered; and I will turn my hand against the little ones.'" [4] In a similar way, Micah testifies that He who would be the judge of Israel struck on the cheek, and who

---
[4] Zech. 13:7

should be born in Bethlehem, was the One "whose goings out are from of old, from ancient times."[5] In other words, the holy Babe of Bethlehem and the eternal Son who was before all things, are one and the same person.

Nor can the prophet's words in Isaiah 50 be made to support any other conclusion. He who came to redeem the world could say, "Behold, at my rebuke I dry up the sea. I make the rivers a wilderness...I clothe the heavens with blackness. I make sackcloth their covering."[6] It is not a different person, but the very same, who goes on to declare: "The Lord GOD has given me the tongue of those who are taught, that I may know how to sustain with words him who is weary"[7]; and who further adds: "I gave my back to those who beat me, and my cheeks to those who plucked off the hair. I didn't hide my face from shame and spitting."[8] In this solemn chapter, He who of old had dried up the Red Sea and driven back the waters of the Jordan river is shown to be identical with Him who on earth had the plucked cheeks, the beaten back, and faced the mockery of humilation! All and only fulfilled in the God-Man Jesus Christ, He who is both the Root *and* the Offspring of David.[9]

There are many other Old Testament passages which at first glance might not seem to refer to the Son, but which the Holy Spirit makes plain in the New Testament, and uses to declare His eternal power and Godhead. A good example of this are the many quotations applied to the Lord Jesus in the first chapter of Hebrews.

Passing over the opening verses—which are meaningless if they are not to be understood as maintaining the full equality of the Son with the Father—we find in Hebrews 1:6 that Psalm 97:7 is to have its fulfillment "when he again brings in the firstborn into the world;"[10] that is, when God sends Jesus the second time, "whom heaven must receive until the times of restoration of all things, which God spoke long ago by the mouth of his holy prophets."[11]

---

[5]Mic. 5:2   [6]Isa. 50:2,3   [7]Isa. 50:4   [8]Isa 50:6   [9]See Rev. 22:16.   [10]Heb. 1:6
[11]Acts 3:21

This throws a flood of light upon Psalm 97. It now becomes clear that it is a millennial hymn of praise upon the return of the once rejected Jesus to exercise His great power and to reign on the throne of David. Verse 7 of Psalm 97, in the original Hebrew language, is *'Worship him, all you gods!'* which the Greek Septuagint (the version the Apostle Paul chooses to quote from when writing Hebrews 1:6) renders as *'all you angels'*. Jesus himself affirmed what was written in the Law: "you shall worship the Lord your God, and you shall serve him only."[12] Obviously then, when God the Father calls upon all angelic beings—good *and* evil—to bow in worship at the feet of Jesus, He is asserting in the fullest possible way Jesus' true deity. Even if all other proofs were insufficient, this here is incontestable evidence that in Jesus we see *'God manifest in flesh.'*

But the other passages quoted are equally striking. Hebrews 1:8–9 shows us that it was "of the Son" the Father was speaking in Psalm 45, which is described as "verses for the king". There, verses 6 and 7 are addressed to Jesus. "Your throne, God, is forever and ever. A sceptre of equity is the sceptre of your kingdom. You have loved righteousness, and hated wickedness. Therefore God, your God, has anointed you with the oil of gladness above your fellows."[13] The first verse asserts His true Godhead. The second, the reality of His manhood. It is the *'mystery of godliness'* in all its preciousness.

The next quotation in Hebrews 1 might never have been noticed in its true prophetic application, were it not for the Holy Spirit's use of it here. In Psalm 102, we have the suffering Saviour, undergoing the agonies of the cross. According to the heading, the psalm is the "prayer of the afflicted, when he is overwhelmed and pours out his complaint before the LORD." In verse 7 He touchingly portrays His fragile condition when He was "like a sparrow that is alone on the housetop." In verse 23,

---

[12] Luke 4:8   [13] Psa. 45:6,7. Charles Russel, founder of the Watch Tower Society and author of a series entitled *'Millennial Dawn'* (later known as *'Studies in the Scriptures'*) frequently denied the use of the Greek *'ho theos'* (God, with the definite article) as being applied to Christ, in his attempts to deny the divinity of Jesus. But it is used in Heb. 1:8, which the author applies specifically to Jesus. Error is never consistent.

He says "He weakened my strength along the course. He shortened my days." And in the first clause of verse 24, He adds "I said, 'My God, don't take me away in the middle of my days."

Now, in most of our English Bibles, the quotation marks do not close, and the next words apparently finish the thought of verse 24. However, according to the inspired use of the passage in Hebrews 1, a period and closing quotation mark should follow what has just been quoted, for the next words are seen to be the answer of God to the holy Sufferer's cry. "'You, Lord, in the beginning, laid the foundation of the earth. The heavens are the works of your hands. They will perish, but you continue. They all will grow old like a garment does. You will roll them up like a mantle, and they will be changed; but you are the same. Your years won't fail.'" [14]

What amazing insight into the mystery of godliness here! The anguished Sufferer on the cross is the One who laid the foundation of the earth, and whose years shall never fail! This is the consistent testimony of Scripture.

NEW TESTAMENT REALITY

If we turn to Matthew 1:23, the virgin's son—Jesus Christ—is given the name "Immanuel, which is, being interpreted, 'God with us.'" Mark takes care to show us that John the Baptizer, in preparation for the ministry of Jesus Christ, was sent to "make ready the way of the Lord!" [15] It is a quotation from Isaiah 40:3 where "the Lord" speaks of Jehovah God. Who else than He could baptize with the Holy Spirit? [16] Think of a creature, even the greatest of all creatures, attempting to do so! It would be to make Deity subservient to creaturehood.

The angel Gabriel's message to Zacharias, as recorded by Luke, coincides with this affirmation of Jesus' identity. Of his son John it is declared that "he will turn many of the children of Israel to the Lord their God. He will go before him in the spirit and power of Elijah..." [17] Read that excerpt carefully. *He will go*

---

[14]Heb. 1:10–12, quoting Psa. 102:24–27.   [15]Mark 1:3   [16]See Mark 1:8.   [17]Luke 1:16,17

before him'—before whom? What other antecedent expression can the pronoun *'him'* refer to except *'the Lord their God'*? Oh, how marvelously do angels, prophets, and apostles, with holy men and women of all times, unite to ascribe the highest honour to the Crucified One, and testify that in Him is revealed this wondrous secret of godliness!

The entire Gospel of John shines with this truth of all truths. Every chapter bears witness to it. The first chapter starts with the oft-quoted statement that "in the beginning was the Word, and the Word was with God, and the Word was God. The same was in the beginning with God."[18] Here, His eternity of being, distinctness of person, unity of nature, and eternal Sonship, are all upheld.   And it was the same uncreated Creator, who "became flesh, and lived amongst us."[19] He was as truly man as He was God.   Nathaniel came to see this, at the end of the chapter, and adoringly cries, "Rabbi, you are the Son of God! You are King of Israel!"[20]

In the second chapter, He asserts His deity when He says to the Jews: "Destroy this temple, and in three days I will raise it up."[21] Deity was dwelling in His body, and when that temple would be destroyed, He would raise it again of His own power. What creature could speak like that without blaspheming? John 3:16—Martin Luther's so-called *'miniature Bible'*—makes known to Nicodemus that He who was supposed to be, at best, "a teacher come from God"[22] is really "his one and only Son,"[23] and therefore one with Him in life and nature.

We will refrain from going chapter to chapter through John at this point, and leave that to your personal study. Let's just pause to note that He who could say "before Abraham came into existence, I AM"[24] could be none other than that holy, holy, holy Lord God of Armies whose glory Isaiah saw,[25] as John 12:41 declares: "Isaiah said these things when he saw his glory, and spoke of him." He it was who "came from God, and was going to God"[26] and who could speak so familiarly to His Father

---

[18]John 1:1,2   [19]John 1:14   [20]John 1:49   [21]John 2:19   [22]John 3:2   [23]John 3:16
[24]John 8:58   [25]See Isa. 6.   [26]John 13:3

of "the glory which I had with you before the world existed." [27]
Is it any wonder that Thomas, convinced at last of truth he had
long doubted, cries out in a holy exclamation "My Lord and my
God!" [28] Notice that he is not rebuked by Jesus, which he should
have been, if he were applying the titles of Deity to a mere
creature. The angels of God refuse to receive worship; [29] but
Jesus accepted it because He "is over all, God, blessed forever." [30]

From the remaining scriptures of the New Testament—of which
it can be truly said, like was said of the temple in times past,
"everything says, 'Glory!'" [31]—we will examine only three
passages, before continuing on to consider the next great
mystery that requires our attention.

Let's notice first the touching words of 2 Corinthians 8:9; "For
you know the grace of our Lord Jesus Christ, that though he was
rich, yet for your sakes he became poor, that you through his
poverty might become rich."

Let those who deny the eternal Sonship of our blessed Lord,
and blasphemously insist that He is only a common creature,
whose existence began when He was born in Bethlehem, tell us
when He was ever rich down here?! "He was rich," *but when?*
Poverty surrounded His lowly birth. In the words of Robert
Chapman (1803–1902): [32]

> *His life of pain and sorrow,*
> *Was like unto His birth,*
> *He would no glory borrow,*
> *No majesty from earth.*

His childhood and young adulthood were not spent amid
wealth and luxury; and as He went about on His mission of love,
He was poorer than the beasts and the birds, for He had no place
to lay His head. At last He died in disgrace and shame on a
criminal's cross, and was hastily laid in a borrowed tomb.

Throughout history, and still today, there have been various
"Christian" groups and teachers who deny the pre-existence of
Christ. The question they fail to answer, is: *when was He rich?*

---

[27]John 17:5   [28]John 20:28   [29]See Rev. 22:8,9.   [30]Rom. 9:5   [31]Psa. 29:9   [32]From
the hymn *'No Bone of Thee Was Broken'*.

There is no other answer if the truth is not acknowledged that He was rich in the glory that He had with the Father in the past eternity, when He, who was "existing in the form of God, didn't consider equality with God a thing to be grasped."[33] That's when He was rich! The next verses show the poverty to which He descended: He "emptied himself, taking the form of a servant, being made in the likeness of men. And being found in human form, he humbled himself, becoming obedient to the point of death, yes, the death of the cross."[34]

In Colossians 1 there is a passage that, due the way some of our English Bibles translate the verse, the full force of the phrase is often obscured. It can accurately be rendered: "For all the fullness was pleased to dwell in him."[35] The context makes it plain that it is the divine Fullness the apostle is referring to. All the fullness of the triune Godhead dwelt in Jesus. Of what creature could this be said, however holy and exalted they may be? It is the unique glory of Him who "is the image of the invisible God, the firstborn of all creation." ('Firstborn' is not, in Scripture, as we might think, always the one born first. It is the pre-eminent one, and the heir. So our Lord Jesus, as Head over all things, is the firstborn of all creation—everywhere supreme.) "For by him all things were created in the heavens and on the earth, visible things and invisible things, whether thrones or dominions or principalities or powers. All things have been created through him and for him. He is before all things, and in him all things are held together."[36]

Lastly, for now, consider the scene laid out in Revelation 5. The Lamb once slain is seen there in the midst of the throne of God—a place no creature shall ever take. The moment He takes the book of judgment, all the redeemed, together with angels and all other created beings, fall down before the Lamb and worship Him as Saviour and Lord. It is the universal recognition of His glory, and is a wondrous and glorious picture.

---

[33]Phil. 2:6   [34]Phil. 2:7,8   [35]Col. 1:19   [36]Col. 1:15–17

Could anything more be needed to show that everyone will recognize the supreme Object of worship to be Him? If He is not God, heaven will be filled with idolaters! But with souls bought by His blood, and minds illuminated by the word of God, every saint joins in offering the once-slain Lamb all homage and adoration, worship and glory and blessing, both now and throughout eternity.

Honest believers can't help but confess the greatness of the *'mystery of godliness'*.   God has been manifested in flesh; divinity and humanity will nevermore be separated.

If anyone denies this truth, they are to be refused as an *antichrist.* As John warns in his second epistle, "don't receive him into your house, and don't welcome him, for he who welcomes him participates in his evil deeds." [37]

Dear fellow believer, please realize God cannot tolerate neutrality when the doctrine of Christ is in question. Oh that His beloved people everywhere were awakened to the importance of standing without compromise for this most fundamental truth, now so frequently and openly denied even amongst professing Christians!

---

[37] 2 John 1:10, 11

CHAPTER 7

The Mystery of the Rapture of the Saints

"Behold, I tell you a mystery. We will not all sleep."[1]

WHAT an amazing statement Paul makes, especially in light of the pronouncement made over and over again by preachers everywhere that we will all die.

'We will,' they say. 'We will not,' says the apostle, by the Holy Spirit's direction. Here then is a mystery deserving our careful consideration, in view of the grave discrepancy between the teaching of the Bible and the general belief of Christendom.

It is only in the epistles of Paul that we can find the revelation of this mystery. Paul was the special witness commissioned by the Lord to make the heavenly calling known. The other twelve apostles were, as we have seen, connected primarily with the testimony to Israel. However Paul, like a "child born at the wrong time,"[2] was selected to be the messenger to the nations, announcing the distinctive truths of this present dispensation.

The Lord Jesus clearly instructed His disciples concerning His second coming—in glory—to destroy His enemies, and to set up His world kingdom. After the Lord's ascension, this was proclaimed everywhere, as His heralds go around making known His gospel. It was also understood that before that Day should come, Israel would experience a period of unparalleled tribulation, which Jeremiah calls "the time of Jacob's trouble."[3]

---

[1]1 Cor. 15:51   [2]1 Cor. 15:8   [3]Jer. 30:7—See Appendix B.

As the time of trouble finishes, the Lord was to appear, to bring in the long-promised reign of peace. All this was in full alignment with the teaching of the Old Testament as to "the sufferings of Christ, and the glories that would follow them."[4]

In order to make this clearer to the reader who may not have given enough attention to these important subjects in the past, or to whom this subject is new, let's briefly consider the Old Testament prophecies and what they revealed, but to a greater extent than in our first chapter. This will involve referring to a large number of Scripture passages, too many to quote in full, but it is hoped that the reader will take the time to look up any verses that they find unfamiliar.

OLD TESTAMENT REVELATION

First, then, let it be noted that Old Testament prophecy never refers to the dispensation in which we currently live (extending from Pentecost in Acts 2 to the Lord's coming for His own) except in a most indefinite way, as, for instance, in Daniel 9:26, a passage which we will address a little farther down.

From Moses to Malachi, Scripture is mainly occupied with one nation: Israel (Amos 3:2; Deuteronomy 7:6; Psalm 147:19,20), and the hope of that nation, namely the raising up of the Prophet (Deuteronomy 18:15), Priest (Psalm 110:4; Zechariah 6:13), and King (Isaiah 32:1; Psalm 2:6), who is to bring them into everlasting blessing as a people (Psalm 132:11–18; Isaiah 35:10; 51:11; 61:7), though not until their regeneration (Ezekiel 36:24-30).

The Gentile will share in that blessing (Isaiah 56:6; 65:1), though not on equal footing with Israel, but rather in subjection to them (Isaiah 14:1–3; 60:3–5; 62:1,2).

The prophets did predict, however, that before the inauguration of the Day of Jehovah's power and Messiah's glory, there would be a rejection of both the awaited Redeemer (Isaiah 53) and the nation of Israel (Isaiah 50). The former rejected by Israel to whom He came; and the latter themselves set aside by God because of having refused His Son when He came in

---

[4] 1 Pet. 1:11

grace to offer Himself to them as both their Lord and their Saviour (Zechariah 7:13,14). Meanwhile, the rejected Messiah takes His place in the heavens on Jehovah's throne (Psalm 110:1), which He will occupy until the future repentance of the people (Hosea 5:15).

This abandonment of Israel however, is not final, as we have seen when looking at the mystery of the olive tree. The 30th and 31st chapters of Jeremiah (detailed commentary on these chapters has been included in Appendix B for further study) together with many other portions of the Word, make this plain. But, they must pass through the time of trouble referred to above, prior to their restoration to divine favor.

Once this period of discipline comes to a conclusion, a remnant will be ready to acknowledge the Crucified Jesus as Israel's Messiah, and "mourn for him, as one mourns for his only son, and will grieve bitterly for him, as one grieves for his firstborn."[5] (Zechariah 12:10-14; 13:6,9) In the darkest hour of their sorrow, when Jerusalem is surrounded by hostile armies, and Israel situation is dire, He will appear as their Deliverer, and the destroyer of their enemies. The tabernacle of David will then be set up again, and the reign of righteousness established (Zechariah 14; Amos 9:8-15). At His coming He is to appear with "all the holy ones."[6] Who these *'holy ones'* are, whether men or angels, is not disclosed here. The appointed time had not yet come to reveal it.

NEW REVELATION

We should now have a solid grasp of the prophetic reach of the Old Testament. Turning to the New Testament, we find fresh information introduced, without which, the present working of the Spirit of God in the world would be impossible to explain.

Keeping in mind what we have learned of the mystery in Romans 11, we see how Israel's rejection has become a way for unforeseen grace to be shown to the nations, though the apostle quotes Old Testament promises of blessing to the heathen as

---

[5]Zech. 12:10   [6]Zech. 14:5

proof that this is compatible with, and not in opposition to, the word of God previously made known. This special work amongst the Gentiles however, is not to continue forever. For if they don't continue in the divine goodness shown them, they too shall be cut off, and the natural branches grafted in, "for God is able to graft them in again."[7]

He is now doing a work unmentioned in the Jewish oracles during the time that His earthly people are called "Lo-Ammi,"[8] and unacknowledged by their God. "A partial hardening has happened to Israel, until the fullness of the Gentiles has come in."[9] The Lord Jesus confirms this (from the political side) in His prophecy of the destruction of Jerusalem and the long period of Gentile supremacy following it, finally culminating in His personal appearing (Luke 21). In Luke 21:24 we read, "Jerusalem will be trampled down by the Gentiles, until the times of the Gentiles are fulfilled."

At first glance, it might be supposed that *the fullness of the Gentiles* synchronizes chronologically with the fulfillment of *the times of the Gentiles.* But it is here that an important distinction is made by the revelation of the mystery of the rapture, which will be exposed as we proceed.

DANIEL'S SEVENTY WEEKS

In order to properly set the stage, read through Daniel 9, and carefully note what is recorded at the end of the chapter concerning Gabriel's prophecy of *the seventy weeks.* We won't attempt a lengthy exposition of this passage here, but will briefly notice the main points. The Lord distinguishes a certain period of time: seventy weeks. The word translated "weeks" is literally *sevens*, which can mean a group of seven days or seven years. The unique form in the original Hebrew, and the subsequent record of history, lead most Biblical scholars to conclude that *seven years* is the intended meaning. Thus the decree of the Lord sets apart 70 times 7, or 490 prophetic years specifically for Daniel's people—the Jewish nation.

---

[7]Rom. 11:23   [8]Hos. 1:9 — meaning, *not my people.*   [9]Rom. 11:25

Before this length of time expires, six important events will have taken place:

1. *Disobedience will be finished;*
2. *An end will be made of sins;*
3. *Atonement[10] will be made for iniquity;*
4. *Everlasting righteousness will be brought in;*
5. *Supernatural visions and prophecies of the future will be finished (all fulfilled);*
6. *The most holy, or the holy of holies, of the millennial temple at Jerusalem will be anointed.[11]*

The seventy weeks are divided into three unequal periods:

First—*seven weeks, or 49 years;*
Second—*sixty-two weeks, or 434 years;*
Third—*one week, or 7 years.*

During the first seven weeks, the streets and walls of the city of Jerusalem were to be restored. The date from which to start counting is found in the second chapter of Nehemiah, in approximately 445 BC, when the cupbearer to Artaxerxes is given permission to return to Jerusalem to rebuild. While no direct commandment is recorded there, Nehemiah 2:12 makes it clear that Nehemiah was following the Lord's direction and under His protection.

The sixty-two weeks seem to have immediately followed, and ended in the coming of the Messiah.[12] At the conclusion of this period, He was cut off and had nothing—but by this, atonement was made for iniquity. Then comes in the present long interval of Jerusalem's down-trodden state. The city is destroyed, as our Lord foretold, and "war will be even to the end," until one arises who confirms a covenant with the majority of Jews for the final, last week. Clearly then, this week is still future. The prophetic

---

[10] A better translation than *'reconciliation.'*   [11] See Ezek. chapters 40–48 for a description of the temple to be rebuilt, and its millennial glory.   [12] Note that the prophetic years may not align directly with our calendar years of 365¼ days. Prophetic scripture appears to utilize 360-day years. Compare Rev. 11:2 (42 months) with Rev. 11:3 (1,260 days) and Dan. 7:25 (3½ times or years).

clock, as noted before, stopped at Calvary. It will not start again "until the fullness of the Gentiles has come in." [13]

This present era is one of an unrevealed duration, [14] parenthetically introduced between the sixty-ninth and seventieth weeks, in which God is taking out from amongst the Gentiles, a people for His name. [15] Not that He has completely abandoned the Jew now, but both Jew and Gentile stand on the same footing: "there is no distinction, for all have sinned." [16] Both can be saved through faith in Christ, and all believers are made members of the one body, the church, by the Holy Spirit, and are united to the Lord Jesus Christ as our Head in heaven, according to the revelation of the mystery which we have already considered.

The church began with the baptism of the Holy Spirit on the day of Pentecost. How long will it exist on earth? Will it remain here throughout "the time of Jacob's trouble," and until the times of the Gentiles are fulfilled?

Scripture answers, *No!* Another mystery was made known to the apostle Paul, declaring the close of the church's history by a mighty miracle which may take place at any moment.

He writes in 1 Corinthians 15:51,52: "Behold, I tell you a mystery. We will not all sleep, but we will all be changed, in a moment, in the twinkling of an eye, at the last trumpet. For the trumpet will sound and the dead will be raised incorruptible, and we will be changed."

This is the true hope of every Christian believer, and it is this marvelous event which marks the *'fullness of the Gentiles.'* The *'times of the Gentiles'* however, will not end until the tribulation period is over, which begins after the rapture of the church. The church will not remain on the earth through that time of trouble. It belongs to heaven, and will be taken home to glory before the great tribulation begins.

---

[13]Rom. 11:25   [14]See Matt. 24:36.   [15]See Acts 15:14.   [16]Rom. 3:22,23

A TIME OF JUDGMENT

In order that this may be made plain to every reader, let's briefly note the characteristics of that tribulation period—a period of judgment. It will be a short dispensation, during which divine wrath will be poured out upon Israel, apostate Christendom, and the nations at large. It is to be the awful result of the rejection of the Prince of Peace.

Revelation 4 through Revelation 19 is focused entirely on the solemn events of that period. Notice the promise given to the church in Revelation 3:10: "because you kept my command to endure, I also will keep you from the hour of testing which is to come on the whole world, to test those who dwell on the earth." In fulfillment of this promise, the heavenly saints are seen enthroned in heaven (represented by the twenty-four elders), [17] who have been redeemed by the blood of the Lamb, before the storm of judgment breaks. Then, when it is all over, they ride forth as a heavenly army with the "Word of God" [18] at His glorious appearing, no longer seen as worshipping, crowned *priests*; but now as *warrior-saints*. This aligns with Zechariah's prophetic declaration, "Yahweh my God will come, and all the holy ones with you." [19]

In the time of trouble and woe that intervenes, the Antichrist "comes in his own name," [20] and will be falsely received by the apostates of Judah and Christendom as the Messiah. The Roman Empire will have been revived in a new and dreadful form by direct satanic energy and Babylon the Great will control it, until judged by God for her blasphemies and her abominable wickedness. The seals will be opened, the trumpets of judgment sounded, and the bowls of wrath poured out. During all this, people will remain unrepentant of their deeds, blaspheming the God of heaven instead. This is the great tribulation.

But we search in vain for any mention of the church or the heavenly saints on earth during that fearful time. *No!* They are above it all—with the Lamb who redeemed them, and who will have taken them to be with Himself.

---

[17] See Rev. 4:10. [18] See Rev. 19:11–16. [19] Zech. 14:5 [20] John 5:43

CAUGHT UP

How, and in what manner, the rapture will take place is clearly
described in 1 Thessalonians 4:13–18. Some in Thessalonica had
been put to sleep by Jesus. Their living brethren feared for them,
assuming that their absence meant they would miss the glory of
the kingdom. Writing to assure their hearts, the apostle says "we
don't want you to be ignorant, brothers, concerning those who
have fallen asleep, so that you don't grieve like the rest, who have
no hope. For if we believe that Jesus died and rose again, even so
God will bring with him those who have fallen asleep in Jesus."

But how can this be, since they have passed away in death?
The *mystery* explains it. God will bring them with Jesus at His
glorious appearing, because He will first raise them up, and then
change the living, *prior to* the appearing in splendor to establish
the kingdom. "For this we tell you by the word of the Lord, that
we who are alive, who are left until the coming of the Lord, will
in no way precede those who have fallen asleep. For the Lord
himself will descend from heaven with a shout, with the voice of
the archangel and with God's trumpet. The dead in Christ will
rise first, then we who are alive, who are left, will be caught up
together with them in the clouds, to meet the Lord in the air. So
we will be with the Lord forever. Therefore comfort one another
with these words."

This is the mystery of the rapture. The shout of the Lord will
awaken all the sleeping church, the voice of the archangel
(Michael, who is the prince of Israel)[21] will summon the saints
of previous dispensations from their tombs, the trumpet of God
will sound[22] finishing this dispensation, and in a moment, all
the redeemed, whether *raised* or *changed*, shall be caught up
(raptured) to meet the Lord in the air.

This is the consistent testimony of Paul in his epistles, and the
genuine hope of the church of God.

---

[21] See Dan. 12:1.   [22] The same as the last trumpet of 1 Cor. 15:52.

How shocking the boldness (or perhaps the ignorance) of those who declare that we must all die, in light of such an amazing truth as that we have been considering!

Paul has lofty words of commendation for the Thessalonian believers who weren't resigned to an inevitable death, but chose instead to "wait for his Son from heaven, whom he raised from the dead: Jesus, who delivers us from the wrath to come."[23] May we each follow their faithful example and likewise wait in hope for the shout and the trumpet blast that will summon us into the presence of our Beloved!

---

[23] 1 Thess. 1:9,10

CHAPTER 8

The Mystery of Lawlessness

*B*LESSED and holy have been the mysteries of God we have contemplated so far. The next one however, is dark and sinister. In fact it is so fearful, that it would seem, at first sight, quite improper to classify it in any sense as amongst the mysteries of God. And yet it is correct to do so, because of all the secrets, none is more difficult for humanity to comprehend than God's toleration of such great evil. Yet not only has He permitted its existence, but He warned us of it beforehand, and foretold its end.

The overarching theme of the first letter Paul wrote to the Thessalonians is the coming of the Lord *for* His saints, while the main theme of the second epistle is His return in majestic glory *with* them. The time span between these two distinct prophetic events will see the *mystery of lawlessness* (or *secret of iniquity*) become fully developed. However, this lawlessness does not appear for the first time during that period as something new —quite the opposite. Even during Paul's own lifetime, when Christianity was still in its infancy, the apostle made the observation in 2 Thessalonians 2:7 that "the mystery of lawlessness already works." That is, this lawlessness is already active and operating effectively in this world. Side by side with the faithful proclamation of the truth has always been satanic work, intentionally and energetically carried out, to corrupt the truth and introduce poisonous counterfeits that delude the souls of all who receive them.

We have already seen this reality symbolically portrayed in Christ's parables of the enemy sowing darnel weeds amongst the wheat, and the woman hiding the leaven in the food of the people of God—the three measures of meal. The same thing is also identified in the letter to Thyatira, where the false prophetess Jezebel is implanting her wicked teachings into the minds of her disciples.[1]

Satan always works by imitation. God has revealed holy mysteries to His servants. The devil too must have his deep things, which appeal to the spiritually proud and carnally-minded. In fact, the *mystery of lawlessness* is the working of the human mind—energized by Satan—in divine things. Refusing the trustworthy and sure testimony of the Lord,[2] and walking in vain confidence, the ear is readily given to fables, and the mind revels in wonderful and strange teachings which delight and bewilder—though in reality are not only unprofitable, they are actually damaging to those who run greedily after them.

Satan's objective is to turn our eyes from Christ. Therefore the mystery of lawlessness exalts mankind, and, by any means whatsoever, puts the Lord Jesus at a distance. And this is successfully accomplished by falsely imitating scriptural truths. Were he to employ a different strategy, it would surely be noticed and raise alarm bells for even the least discerning. So we are told that "even as Jannes and Jambres opposed Moses,[3] so these also oppose the truth, men corrupted in mind, who concerning the faith are rejected."[4] Therefore, to trace out the progress of this dark and dreadful mystery, we must look for some gigantic systematizing of error—a counterfeiting of divine truths.

TRUTH COUNTERFEITED

We don't have to look very far, for from the beginning it is only too evident. In its earliest inception, this mystery consisted in assuming the hopes, ordinances and ceremonies of the Jewish dispensation, and transferring them gradually to the church of the present age. With this accomplished, the heavenly calling would be lost sight of, the great mystery of Christ and the

---

[1]See Rev. 2:18–23. [2]See Psa. 19:7. [3]By imitating the miracles Aaron performed in front of Pharaoh. See Exo. 7:11. [4]2 Tim. 3:8

church would be effectively hidden, and believers would sink down to the level of the world, becoming, in effect, *dwellers on the earth*[5] and forgetting that their citizenship is in heaven.[6]

It was not a matter of great difficulty to persuade those who were formerly Jews and heathen, used to religious structure and sacred ceremonies, that a Christianity without much outward attractiveness was inferior to ornate and elaborate rituals. Consequently, we soon see the truth of the priesthood of all believers (each and every believer has immediate access to God) displaced by the teaching that, as in Judaism and in heathenism, so now, there is a special priestly order who alone can deal directly with the mysteries of religion, and who act as mediators and intermediary representatives for the laity, or the common people.

This was one of Satan's most cunning tricks to put the people at a distance from God, and how successful it has been over the centuries! Slowly but surely, more and more power, with its accompanying glamour, was delegated to this superior hierarchy—fancy clothes were adopted, magnificent titles invented—with the result that the simple Christianity of early days seemed almost crushed out of existence. Priestly functions also extended farther and farther. Baptism became a sacrament only to be administered by this special class, who were also the only ones holy enough to dispense the elements of the Lord's Supper, to solemnize a marriage, to anoint the sick, and to hear confessions of sin (with the power to grant forgiveness!).

The ordinance of baptism itself became mysterious; instead of a testimony of symbolic identification with the crucified and risen Christ, the baptismal waters were now understood to wash away the stain of original sin, and cause the regeneration and rebirth of the one baptized. The simple *'breaking of bread'* was replaced by the mysterious and blasphemous sacrifice of the mass—a continual and unbloody sacrifice for the sins of the living and the dead! Anointing the sick with oil by the elders of

---

[5] The expression *'dwellers on the earth'* refers, not to all who live in the world, but to a distinct moral class characterized by earthly-mindedness. This is addressed further in Appendix A.

[6] See Phil. 3:20.

the church, that they might be healed in answer to prayer, became the sacrament of extreme unction to prepare the doubting, bewildered soul for death, instead of life! Christ Himself as the "one mediator between God and men"[7] was largely replaced by so-called *'saints'* (made so after their death by hierarchial authority) and *'the holy Virgin'* more accessible than her divine Son! Thus, one by one, doctrines and usages were so perverted they became unrecognizable.

Suffice it to say that the working of this mystery has been so effective that there is not one doctrine of Scripture remaining that has not been denied, and a false imitation imposed on the spiritually ignorant in its place. Thus it went on spreading, not only through the Roman Catholic church, but amongst so-called Greek orthodox, and more recently amongst Anglican and even Protestant denominations, as well as heretical sects like Christian Science, New Thought, and others.

FUTURE LAWLESSNESS

But this lawlessness is not yet fully grown, nor will it be, while the church, indwelt by the Holy Spirit, remains on the earth.

In 2 Thessalonians 2, we read of a present-day restraint that is preventing the full manifestation of the evil of the mystery of lawlessness. This is evidently the presence of the Holy Spirit in the church on earth. He "restrains now, until he is taken out of the way."[8] When the Spirit goes up with the church at the Lord's descent into the air, "then the lawless one will be revealed, whom the Lord will kill with the breath of his mouth, and destroy by the manifestation of his coming; even he whose coming is according to the working of Satan with all power and signs and lying wonders, and with all deception of wickedness for those who are being lost, because they didn't receive the love of the truth, that they might be saved. Because of this, God sends them a working of error, that they should believe a lie; that they all might be judged who didn't believe the truth, but had pleasure in unrighteousness."[9]

---

[7] 1 Tim. 2:5   [8] 2 Thess. 2:7   [9] 2 Thess. 2:8–12

This is certainly a most solemn passage, and it deserves to be considered carefully. It refers to events which may take place very, very soon—a state of affairs many living now may soon find themselves facing. The more it is examined in detail, the more clearly it will be seen that it portrays a terrible period, soon to come upon all that live on the earth. The church will be gone, the mystery of lawlessness will be headed up in one man—the *Antichrist* of prophecy—and all who have chosen the earth in place of the heavenly portion will be given over to strong delusion.

This removes all hope of any being saved in that coming "hour of testing" [10] who have heard the gospel of the grace of God in this "day of salvation" [11] but heard it only to reject it. It puts a terrible responsibility on those who listen again and again to the proclamation of salvation through faith in the Lord Jesus Christ, yet have never trusted Him for themselves. Instead they have either continued on in their sins in utter indifference, or else believe that by trusting in either their church affiliation, a human priesthood, or religious practices, they have made their peace with God—thus ignoring Christ who alone made peace by the blood of His cross.

It is truly sobering to realize that if Christ should come to call His own away while they are in this awful state, they will be left for certain judgment, for God Himself will send the delusion, or "working of error," which will destine them to judicial darkness. In this dispensation of grace, they "loved the darkness rather than the light; for their works were evil." [12] Then, in that time of deepest distress, they will be given up to the darkness they have loved and deliberately chosen.

This, of course, is not unprecedented in history. There are previous instances of God's sending men delusions and visiting them with judicial blindness. Refer to the cases of Pharaoh (Exodus 11:10), of Ahab (2 Chronicles 18), and of the nation of Israel (Isaiah 6:9,10; Matthew 13:13–15).

---

[10]Rev. 3:10   [11]2 Cor. 6:2   [12]John 3:19

All who hear the gospel and don't believe it are already under condemnation.[13] If the Lord comes while they are still in that state, the condemnation is final.   Second Thessalonians 1 describes their dreadful doom, together with the contrast of the blessed position that might have been theirs had they only believed the testimony so graciously given, "when the Lord Jesus is revealed from heaven with his mighty angels in flaming fire, punishing those who don't know God, and to those who don't obey the Good News of our Lord Jesus, who will pay the penalty: eternal destruction from the face of the Lord and from the glory of his might, when he comes in that day to be glorified in his saints and to be admired amongst all those who have believed."[14] There could be no stronger declaration that all who reject the testimony of Christ now, will be unable to respond to the testimony then, since the result of the outpouring of divine wrath upon the world will only harden hearts further, instead of bringing them to repentance.[15]

It would seem, from a careful study of the book of Revelation, that immediately following the rapture of the saints, all the Christ-less fragments of Christendom will be united for a time in one universal and worldwide church: Babylon the Great. For not in any past history of Rome has Revelation 17 been completely fulfilled—Babylon, in its final phase, is yet future. There she is seen as the great prostitute reigning for a brief season over many waters, which, it is explained, "are peoples, multitudes, nations, and languages."[16]

Upon her proud forehead is written: "MYSTERY, BABYLON THE GREAT, THE MOTHER OF THE PROSTITUTES AND OF THE ABOMINATIONS OF THE EARTH."[17] She is drunk with the blood of the saints, who in all ages have been killed by the followers of false religions.   She exercises control over the revived Roman empire for a time, until at last she is overthrown and utterly burned with fire by those who had once been her wretched slaves.

And so Babylon's power will be broken, and all worship and

[13] See John 3:18.   [14] 2 Thess. 1:7–10   [15] See Rev. 16:9–11,21.   [16] Rev. 17:15
[17] Rev. 17:5

allegiance will be directed towards a man—"the man of sin"[18]—
who himself embodies the mystery of lawlessness in its entirety.
This is the subject of Revelation 13, which appears to occur after
Revelation 17 chronologically, for there we see no woman riding
the beast. Her doom has already come, and now the man of sin
is fully revealed, and everyone worships the Antichrist, the false
Messiah.

This will be the devil's masterpiece, and the culmination of
the mystery he has been developing for so long. But his triumph
will only be momentary; for when lawlessness is at its height,
and Satan's power seems to be supreme, the glorious scene John
records in Revelation 19 will occur. "I saw the heaven opened,
and behold, a white horse, and he who sat on it is called Faithful
and True. In righteousness he judges and makes war. His eyes
are a flame of fire, and on his head are many crowns. He has
names written and a name written which no one knows but he
himself. He is clothed in a garment sprinkled with blood. His
name is called "The Word of God." The armies which are in
heaven followed him on white horses, clothed in white, pure,
fine linen...I saw the beast, and the kings of the earth, and their
armies, gathered together to make war against him who sat on
the horse, and against his army. The beast was taken, and with
him the false prophet who worked the signs in his sight, with
which he deceived those who had received the mark of the beast
and those who worshipped his image. These two were thrown
alive into the lake of fire that burns with sulphur." [19]

And with that, the mystery of lawlessness will be forever
blotted out and righteousness alone will reign!

---

[18] 2 Thess. 2:3   [19] Rev. 19:11–14, 19, 20

CHAPTER 9

The Mystery of God Finished

*R*EVELATION, the final book of the Bible, is an *apocalypse*. It is not *apocrypha*—that is, something concealed, or hidden—but a disclosure of knowledge; a revealing. It reveals the final dealings of God with humanity on the earth, and it proves His righteousness both in grace and judgment. But it is primarily a book of judgment, specifically as it relates to three distinct groups. Detailed within are the judgments that must fall on apostate Christendom, on disobedient Israel, and on the defiant nations.

The heart of the book is the tenth chapter, and the core of that portion is the angel's declaration that "in the days of the voice of the seventh angel, when he is about to sound, then the mystery of God is finished, as he declared to his servants, the prophets."[1] This is the theme of the book with the seven seals[2] —the vindication of God's holiness in having tolerated evil in His universe for so long. What greater mystery confronts and confuses the human mind than the question of why God allows unrighteousness to triumph so often? It is what people call the *mystery of Providence* but Providence is only another name for God. This is His secret. He will disclose it in the proper time, and all things will be as clear as day. Until then, our faith rests upon His Word, and trusts His love, no matter how true it may seem to be that goodness and righteousness are of little value in

---

[1]Rev. 10:7   [2]See Rev. 5:1.

this present age, and have been since Cain rose up against his brother and killed him.

James Russell Lowell (1819–1891) depicted this in his poem *'The Present Crisis'* with the verse:

> *Careless seems the great Avenger;*
>> *history's pages but record*
> *One death-grapple in the darkness,*
>> *'twixt old systems and the Word;*
> *Truth forever on the scaffold,*
>> *Wrong forever on the throne,—*
> *Yet that scaffold sways the future,*
>> *and behind the dim unknown*
> *Standeth God within the shadow,*
>> *keeping watch above His own.*

God's final triumph over every and all evil is what is so vividly presented in the rapidly shifting scenes of "the Revelation of Jesus Christ, which God gave him to show to his servants the things which must happen soon."[3]

UNDERSTANDING THE REVELATION

The book of Revelation is not as confusing and hard to spiritually comprehend as many imagine it to be. The text divides naturally into three parts, according to the Lord's instructions to John: "Write therefore the things which you have seen, and the things which are, and the things which will happen hereafter."[4] The first division is, of course, the opening chapter, with its account of what John had seen—the glorified Lord Jesus in amongst the assemblies of His people. The things which are—that is, which are in the present, or which are currently going on now—refer to the church-age activities the Lord judges in His letters to the seven assemblies in chapters two and three. The balance of the book is devoted to the third division—the things which will happen after the church's history on earth is finished. It is the time of the end, the short period of judgment, when all who have refused the grace of God

---

[3]Rev. 1:1   [4]Rev. 1:19

will have to know His vengeance. This is in full agreement with what is clearly taught throughout the rest of Scripture.

At the end of the age, the weeds are gathered in bundles and burned;[5] the one not wearing the wedding clothing is cast into outer darkness;[6] the unfaithful servant is appointed his portion with the hypocrites;[7] the foolish virgins, though they go for oil, are shut outside;[8] the unprofitable servant has everything taken away;[9] those who neglected to enter in to the narrow door seek unsuccessfully to enter it then;[10] and people will be like those who refused to be warned by Enoch and Noah and perished in the flood, and those who didn't listen to Lot and were destroyed in Sodom.[11]

These, then, are the ones who become followers of the Antichrist, and are crushed by the wrath of the Lamb!

But it is equally plain that the period described in Revelation 4 through 19 will not be one of unmixed judgment. There are some who will become the objects of sovereign grace, and who, though they pass through the terrible tribulation of that time, will be saved out of it. But these are not those who reject Christ now, whose hearts become soft then, and who embrace the Saviour they now refuse.

In short, we search Scripture in vain for one hint that anyone who rejects the gospel of Christ now will be saved in that day. Nor does the expression we read in Revelation 7:9 disagree with this—"of every nation and of all tribes, peoples, and languages"—for none of Israel will apparently be amongst them, since in that chapter we see the 144,000 of the twelve tribes quite distinct from the great multitude. What the expression really declares is the *universality* of the response to the everlasting gospel amongst the heathen nations; but Christendom, like Israel, is not included, unless there is found even there, some who had never heard the gospel before. This *'everlasting gospel'* is not the gospel of the grace of God as is

---

[5]See Matt. 13:30,40–42.   [6]See Matt. 22:13.   [7]See Matt. 24:48–51.   [8]See Matt. 25:11.   [9]See Matt. 25:28–30.   [10]See Luke 13:24.   [11]See Luke 17:26–30.

now being proclaimed, but the good news that the long reign of lawlessness is almost over, and the Omnipotent Lord God is about to assert His power, and thus the mystery of His toleration of evil shall be solved at last. There will be found in that day a people who will receive this message with conviction, and turn to Him in repentance, confessing their sins.

Furthermore, we are reminded that this will be the period of Israel's awakening, as we have already seen in several passages. In Daniel 12:3 we read the promise that "those who are wise will shine as the brightness of the expanse. Those who turn many to righteousness will shine as the stars forever and ever." This is, as the verses just before explain, during the great time of trouble, but "at that time your people will be delivered, everyone who is found written in the book."[12]

The hour of their darkest trouble and deepest sorrow will result in the elect amongst Israel returning to the Lord. The 144,000 of Revelation 7 are a picture of those who will say, "Come! Let's return to the LORD; for he has torn us to pieces, and he will heal us; he has injured us, and he will bind up our wounds."[13] Zion's painful labours will result in a great birthing of children, as predicted in Micah 5:3, and also in Isaiah 66:8, which says "Who has heard of such a thing? Who has seen such things? Shall a land be born in one day? Shall a nation be born at once? For as soon as Zion travailed, she gave birth to her children." The verses that follow it are also deserving of special attention in this connection. Further prophetic understanding can also be found in Zechariah 12 and 13.

And so their "partial hardening" will end, once the "fullness of the Gentiles has come in,"[14] as also shown in Hosea 3:4,5: "For the children of Israel shall live many days without king, and without prince, and without sacrifice, and without sacred stone, and without ephod or idols. Afterward the children of Israel shall return, and seek the LORD their God, and David their king, and shall come with trembling to the LORD and to

---

[12]Dan. 12:1   [13]Hos. 6:1   [14]Rom. 11:25

his blessings in the last days." This is true, not of the nation as a whole,[15] but of the remnant. The majority will be destroyed for their apostasy and the remnant will be recognized as the nation, "and so all Israel will be saved."[16] Even being one of the sons of Jacob doesn't guarantee an opportunity of grace. No one who refuses the truth now, whether they be Jew or Gentile, can be saved then.

During this time, before the end comes, the gospel of the Kingdom will be preached by the Jews for a witness in all the earth. Sent forth by the Spirit from on high, they will proclaim the coming of the Kingdom far and wide, and urge people to repent as John the Baptizer did so long ago.[17] Thus we see grace going out to the Gentiles who have not heard the truth previously. The great result of this campaign is also seen in Zechariah 8:20–23.

Our Lord's teaching related to the judgment in Matthew 25 aligns with this. These events take place at His coming to the earth. Everyone of the living nations are gathered before Him. He will separate them according to the treatment they gave the Jewish missionaries mentioned above, whom He calls "my brothers."[18] No one is commended for being very spiritually astute, but at least they did not reject or neglect the messengers. They are saved, and enter into the kingdom prepared for them from the foundation of the world. They are those "blessed of my Father."[19]

And so, even though the sword of judgment is unsheathed, grace is still exercised according to His word, "I will have mercy on whom I have mercy, and I will have compassion on whom I have compassion."[20] From Israel and the Gentiles, a countless number will go into the millennial kingdom, and acknowledge the leadership of the blessed One, once made a curse for them, as He was for us. But not one who has rejected the Lamb of God in this present age will be amongst them.

---

[15]See Zech. 13:8,9; Isa. 24:13; Ezek. 20:31–44.   [16]Rom. 11:26   [17]See Matt. 24:14.
[18]Matt. 25:40   [19]Matt. 25:34   [20]Rom. 9:15

There will be some who will be numbered with the heavenly saints after the church is gone. They will be exclusively Jewish, as evidenced by the fact that they sing "the song of Moses, the servant of God, and the song of the Lamb."[21] Through martyrdom under the Beast and Antichrist they lose an earthly inheritance, and obtain a heavenly one. Their part will be, not with the church—the body of Christ and Eve of the last Adam—but no doubt with those of old who "desire a better country, that is, a heavenly one."[22] In Revelation 20 we see them enthroned with the rest who live and reign a thousand years. They will be forever with the Lamb, but won't occupy the special place enjoyed by those who now believe in Him and who are identified with Him in the present hour of His rejection.

THE FULFILLMENT OF REVELATION

Having briefly sketched out the actions of God in judgment and in grace, as laid out in the third great division of the Revelation, let's spend time considering its order in more detail. It seems to divide into two almost equal parts, each of which covers the same time period, only that the latter has Israel more particularly in view, and the former the Gentiles. An appendix is included too, having to do with the church in the glory of God.

The first of these two parts begins in Revelation 4:1 with the door opened in heaven and continues on to the judgment of the wicked dead, ending at Revelation 11:18. The second portion, giving details omitted in the former part, begins with the temple of God opened in heaven (and the ark of His covenant, speaking of His relationship to Israel, seen), in Revelation 11:19, and goes on to the final judgment of Revelation 20. The remainder of the book of Revelation is a kind of appendix, highlighting the glories of the bride, the Lamb's wife, the heavenly Jerusalem.

It will be noticed that in the beginning of the first section, twenty-four crowned priests are seen in heaven, robed in white and sitting on thrones, surrounding the throne of God and the Lamb. These are without question the heavenly saints who have

---

[21]Rev. 15:3   [22]Heb. 11:16

been translated to glory at the coming of the Lord for His own, according to 1 Thessalonians 4 (as seen in the chapter on the Mystery of the Rapture). God is now about to draw His sword for the final conflict, but He takes care to gather His own to Himself before the judgments fall.

In Revelation 5, the Lamb is the only One found worthy to open and look inside the book with seven seals—the title-deeds to the earth that once cast Him out. As fast as He breaks the seals, judgments (against which men harden themselves) fall upon the earth that refused Him, as described in Revelation 6, 8, and 9.

Revelation 7 is a parenthesis, letting us know that, even in that fearful hour of His wrath, a remnant of Israel, and a great multitude of the heathen nations, will (as we have already clearly seen) be saved for the earth, and the earthly aspect of the millennial kingdom.

The opening of the seventh seal releases the entire scroll, and seven angels who stand before God are given seven trumpets. Just as the marching Israelites sounded the trumpets of Jehovah's judgment about Jericho prior to its terrible fall, so these too shall sound the downfall of all that mankind and Satan have built up throughout the ages.

Six of these trumpets sound in Revelation 8 and 9. And, just like the parenthesis that occurred between the sixth and the seventh seal, so here we have another one between the last two trumpets.

The mighty angel of Revelation 10, who comes down from heaven, can be none other than the blessed Lord Himself. What created being could be described that way? He is "clothed with a cloud *(the cloud of the divine glory)*. A rainbow was on his head. His face was like the sun *(supreme majesty)*, and his feet like pillars of fire." [23] Furthermore, He has the now-opened book in His hand, and, as Possessor of all created things, He puts His right foot on the sea, and His left foot on the land. Lifting up His hand to heaven, He "swore by him who lives forever and ever, who created heaven and the things that are in it, the earth and

---

[23] Rev. 10:1

the things that are in it, and the sea and the things that are in it, that there will no longer be delay, but in the days of the voice of the seventh angel, when he is about to sound, then the mystery of God is finished, as he declared to his servants, the prophets." [24]

John is then commanded to eat the book. Prophecy doesn't consist of idle words, or mere intellectual instruction, but is to be received into the heart, that it may enable the believer to live *now* in the light of *then*.

The first fourteen verses of Revelation 11 continue the parenthesis, proclaiming the Lord's care for Jerusalem and His judgment on the apostate portion of the nation. The climax is reached in Revelation 11:15, when the seventh angel sounds his trumpet "and great voices in heaven followed, saying, 'The kingdom of the world has become the Kingdom of our Lord, and of his Christ. He will reign forever and ever!'"

This involves the complete overthrow of Satan's power, therefore destroying all evil, and the bringing in of everlasting righteousness. So the Millennium and the day of judgment at its close are all anticipated. Therefore "the twenty-four elders, who sit on their thrones before God's throne, fell on their faces and worshipped God, saying: 'We give you thanks, Lord God, the Almighty, the one who is and who was; because you have taken your great power and reigned. The nations were angry, and your wrath came, as did the time for the dead to be judged, and to give your bondservants the prophets, their reward, as well as to the saints, and those who fear your name, to the small and the great, and to destroy those who destroy the earth.'" [25]

And so the secret of God will be finished, and evil will appear to be the dark background against which His grace and His holiness will stand out in bolder contrast than if sin had never been permitted to lift up its head in the universe.

---

[24]Rev. 10:6,7   [25]Rev. 11:16–18

As stated previously, the second part of the prophecy covers the same ground, reaching its climax in the judgment of the great white throne. The millennial reign of Christ will be a time of rewards for His saints, and will close with judgment on His adversaries.

This world, in fact the entire universe, may be likened to a business venture which has been destroyed through criminal leadership, and therefore is put under the control of a receiver, so that its affairs may be straightened out. When everything is back in order, the receivership comes to an end.

Our Lord Jesus Christ is the Receiver. Mankind, ruled by Satan, has hopelessly ruined both himself and everything God put under his management. Jesus is given the receivership. He will bring order out of the existing chaos, and put everything right. "Then the end comes, when he will deliver up the Kingdom to God, even the Father, when he will have abolished all rule and all authority and power. For he must reign until he has put all his enemies under his feet. The last enemy that will be abolished is death... When all things have been subjected to him, then the Son will also himself be subjected to him who subjected all things to him, that God may be all in all." [26]

His work of receivership will be successfully completed. Evil banished, righteousness triumphant, the mystery finished, and God—Father, Son, and Holy Spirit—will be all in all throughout an eternity of bliss, in which wickedness shall never again rear its ugly head!

But no one in that unending day of God will sing so sweet a song as those who once were sinners lost and guilty, yes, vile and loathsome too, but who have been saved by divine grace, and shall forever praise the Lamb who died, and extol the precious blood that cleansed from sin's pollution. Had there been no sin, there could have been no Saviour. And oh, how great the loss, to have known our Lord as Sovereign and Creator, but not as the One who died to redeem us to God with

---

[26] 1 Cor. 15:24–26,28

His own blood, binding our hearts to Himself for all the ages to come.

> *One string there is of sweetest tone,*
>   *Reserved for sinners saved by grace;*
> *'Tis sacred to one class alone,*
>   *And touched by one peculiar race.*
> *Though angels may with rapture see*
>   *How mercy flows in Jesus' blood,*
> *It is not theirs to prove, as we,*
>   *The cleansing virtue of this flood.*[27]

---

[27]From the hymn *'How Pleasant is the Sound of Praise'* by Thomas Kelly (1769-1855).

Enemies of the Cross of Christ and Dwellers on the Earth

This is a revision of H.A. Ironside's article that was first published in the 1901 edition of Help and Food for the Household of Faith magazine, and had been included as an Appendix in the original edition of this book to provide evidence that 'earth-dwellers' appear to be a distinct moral class in Scripture.

*A*N attentive reader can scarcely fail to notice that Philippians 3 is a chapter abounding in distinct contrasts.

First, there is the contrast between the Judaizers, whom the apostle contemptuously calls in Greek the *'katatome'* (literally, the cutting off or mutilation) and those whom he designates the *'peritome'* (the cutting around, or circumcision), who have no confidence in the flesh and who rejoice in Christ Jesus (Phil. 3:2,3).

This leads him to contrast his own past religiousness—his trust in the flesh—with his present condition, having counted all things he had gained as loss for Christ and gladly letting everything go by considering it stinking garbage, in order to win Him (Phil. 3:4–9).

The legal righteousness which "is of the law" is contrasted with "the righteousness which is from God by faith" (Phil. 3:9). This is simply continuing on the distinction noticed just above.

Then there is, or at least is implied, the contrast between the resurrection of judgment (*'anastasis'*) which was all he could once look forward to, and the *out*-resurrection (*'exanastasis'*) from amongst the dead, in which he now expects to participate (Phil. 3:10,11).

Perfection (in the sense of absolute holiness) is then contrasted with perfection (or mature growth) in the sense of having apprehended the great truths of the gospel (Phil. 3:12–16). The former he denies having, for sinless perfection will only be ours once raised or changed. Regarding the latter he can say, "Let us therefore, as many as are perfect, think this way."

Lastly, he contrasts the body of our humiliation with the bodies to be ours at the Lord's coming, "conformed to the body of his glory" (Phil. 3:21).

Just before this, however, he points out a contrast between two moral classes that are frequently brought before us in the book of Revelation, and in fact, are distinguished everywhere in Scripture. It is the clear and stark contrast between *earthly-* and *heavenly*-mindedness.

"For many walk, of whom I told you often, and now tell you even weeping, as the enemies of the cross of Christ, whose end is destruction, whose god is the belly, and whose glory is in their shame, who think about earthly things" (Phil. 3:18,19).

In contrast to these, are the heavenly-minded ones: "for our citizenship is in heaven, from where we also wait for a Saviour, the Lord Jesus Christ" (Phil. 3:20). The seventeenth verse should also be noticed in this connection: "Brothers, be imitators together of me, and note those who walk this way, even as you have us for an example" (Phil. 3:17). The *'walking'* here no doubt refers to taking on an outward Christian lifestyle. Those who *'walk'* are those who, presumably at least, are on a pilgrimage. They profess "that they are seeking a country."[1] In the Old Testament we read "the LORD your God ...has known your walking through this great wilderness;"[2] while in Acts 9:31, we are told of the church (foreshadowed symbolically by Israel) that they were "walking in the fear of the Lord and in the comfort of the Holy Spirit." They too had gone out into the desert with God. They were no longer at home here. May our walk through this world be as theirs, "in the fear of the Lord."

---

[1] Heb. 11:14.   [2] Deut. 2:7

Those referred to in Philippians 3:18 had the outward appearance of pilgrims, and yet, unlike those who began with the redemption of which the blood-sprinkled doorposts and the divided sea of the Exodus pictured, they were enemies of the cross of Christ!

There were similar ones who walked with Israel in olden times. The same chapter that presents God's people starting on their journey, after having been sheltered by the blood of the lamb, tells us that "a mixed multitude went up also with them, with flocks, herds, and even very much livestock."[3] Outwardly, perhaps, one might have had difficulty in distinguishing them from the elect nation, but their real character came out in the wilderness. In Numbers 11:4–6, we get the cry of the people who were enemies of the cross of Christ (not literally, but as a figurative type), who had never entered into what the Red Sea judgment should have taught them—separation from Egypt and its lusts: "The mixed multitude that was amongst them lusted exceedingly; and the children of Israel also wept again, and said, 'Who will give us meat to eat? We remember the fish, which we ate in Egypt for nothing; the cucumbers, and the melons, and the leeks, and the onions, and the garlic; but now we have lost our appetite. There is nothing at all except this manna to look at.'" And yet, the *manna* represents Christ come down in grace to meet His people's need.[4] But sadly, His beauty becomes temporarily obscured by associating with those whom the apostle warns us of with tears in Philippians 3, and we begin to lose our appreciation of it, though He be "like wafers with honey"[5] for sweetness, and fresh upon the dew—ministered in the power of the Holy Spirit.

They had no heart for the manna—they would far rather have had the meat and fish of Egypt, and the fruit which they must grovel on the ground to obtain, or even dig into the earth for. So it always is when our souls are no longer drawn to His cross; when we can no longer say, "far be it from me to boast, except in the cross of our Lord Jesus Christ, through which the world has been crucified to me, and I to the world."[6]

---

[3]Exo. 12:38   [4]See John 6:32.   [5]Exo. 16 31   [6]Gal. 6:14

Have we not all known something of the deadening influence of the *mixed multitude* who "walk" and "desire to make a good impression in the flesh,"[7] but whose hearts are still in the world, where they would also like to draw ours? Let us not forget leeks, onions and garlic all leave their odor behind!

You cannot feast on things like these without spiritual loss. Perhaps you have convinced yourself that a little bit of worldliness, a little indulgence of the flesh, will not hurt your testimony, nor interfere with your enjoyment of divine things. You imagine it will never be noticed by other believers, even those whose holy living you have respect for and those leaders who watch out for your soul. After all, if you do allow yourself to indulge in the world a little, you are, at least, regularly out to the church meetings and display an interest in the gospel.

Be assured: it is just as impossible to dine on garlic and not have the odor on your breath, as it is to taste of the world's ungodliness in any form without lowering the tone of your spirituality in an obvious manner. Indulge in earthly vanities, worldly passions and careless ways, and you eat away at your spiritual life and cause your soul to loathe the manna! You cannot enjoy the world and Christ at the same time. One will inevitably crowd the other one out.

It appears that there is a distinction, a notable one, between the *mixed multitude* and *murmuring Israel.* Similarly, we need to distinguish between the "the enemies of the cross of Christ, whose end is destruction" (notice they are not merely being chastened), and the Philippian saints who are being warned against worldliness. For even the saint is in danger of becoming like them in many ways, if unwatchful, although they can never actually be one with them. Believers, sadly, are often forgetful of the cross of Christ, though they cannot be enemies. Still, while our ultimate salvation is never at risk, believer's are admonished in 1 Corinthians 9:24–10:11 to learn from the example of those in the wilderness whose walk displeased God and who had to suffer the consequences of their unfaithfulness.

---

[7] Gal. 6:12

Wisdom's children take heed and are kept safe; but the foolish pass on and are punished.

The telltale characteristic of these "whose glory is in their shame" is *earthly-mindedness*—"whose god is the belly...who think about earthly things." In this, their connection with the mixed multitude is very plain. Lust—the desire for personal gratification, whatever form it may take—and love of the world from which the cross has made the Christian separate, are their two great distinguishing marks.

Let us, dear fellow pilgrim, be wary of anyone who would tempt us to seek our enjoyment in the world that has banished our Lord. His cross has come between us and the world. Do we, then, want anything out of it, or a place in it? If so, in our hearts, we go back to Egypt. Remember, to return, Israel had to go around the Red Sea;[8] they could not go through it like they did the first time with the Lord's mighty hand.

It is an awful thing to set the cross aside. It is not necessarily denying our faith in the death of Christ or in the shedding of His blood. These truths may be acknowledged and confessed in some measure, yet the cross—the symbol of His shame and bitter sorrow—has really been ignored.

It is the cross that has stained all the glory of this world; just as in olden times the cedar wood, the scarlet and the hyssop were stained with the blood of the bird, killed in an earthen vessel over running water[9]—Christ the heavenly One, in the body prepared for Him offered Himself through the eternal Spirit a sacrifice for our cleansing. This world has not had glory since it became guilty of the murder of the Son of God, since it nailed our Lord to the tree. All its objects of beauty, its religious splendor, its society, its culture—everything in which it prides itself—all is blood-stained now.

This is what those "who think about earthly things" deny. Refusing the truth that Christ is outside this arena of man's pride and foolishness, they try to attach His name to the world

---

[8]See Jer. 43:1–7.   [9]See the law for cleansing healed lepers in Lev. 14.

that cast Him out. Back then, they cried, *'Crucify Him!'* Now they attempt to dress up His tomb.

They can't completely ignore Jesus Christ. His impact is too strong and clear for that. It was impossible that God in human form could be in the world and yet not leave some evidence of His presence behind. So instead, they admit to Him, but only as someone like themselves.

Have you noticed that so many are willing to recognize Jesus, even though they hate His cross? They speak of Him as a moral leader, a philosophical teacher, a political martyr, even as their personal inspiration. But that He died to deliver us from this present evil age—that His cross is the dividing line—this they will not have.

In contrast to the many whose interests are on the earth, it is refreshing to read of some whose "citizenship is in heaven." Here on earth, they find no permanent city to call home. They look and wait for one to come. [10] Christ's lonely path of sorrow and separation is the one they also walk in such a world as this. Identified by faith with a rejected Christ, and possessing His life by new birth, they cannot be at home in the world where He experienced His deep, deep sufferings and His awful shame. A separated, holy, and special people, [11] they are content to wait for glory until the future day of His appearing. His narrow path of alienation and persecution is far more rewarding than earth's wide highways. "For you were called to this, because Christ also suffered for us, leaving you an example, that you should follow his steps." [12]

The contrast is distinctly clear now, and it will be at the end too. Caught up to be forever with Himself will be all those who knew Him as Lord and Saviour. Left in the earth of their own choosing and the place of their hopes will be those who were the enemies of His cross. The future of both are outlined in the book of Revelation.

To the assembly that only had a little strength, but who had not denied the name of the absent King, He says, "because you

---

[10]See Heb. 13:14.   [11]See 1 Pet. 2:9.   [12]1 Pet. 2:21

kept my command to endure, I also will keep you from the hour of testing which is to come on the whole world, to test those who dwell on the earth." [13]

These *'earth-dwellers'* are evidently the same moral class as those whose present earthly ways we have been considering. That the expression "those who dwell on the earth" does not refer merely to inhabitants of the world is clear by referring to Revelation 11:9,10 and Revelation 14:6, where we find in both passages they are distinguished from "the peoples, tribes, languages, and nations."

In the verse quoted above (Revelation 3:10) we see that when the Lord comes and takes His own away from the place of their toil and suffering to enter into His own rest in the glory of God, these earth-dwellers will be left behind (despite their possible Christian profession) [14] to pass through the terrible period of judgment depicted so graphically in this closing portion of the oracles of God.

That they are identical with the false professors of every age is clear from Revelation 6:10 where we hear the martyrs crying for their blood to be avenged "on those who dwell on the earth." As the enemies of the cross of Christ, they have been over and over again the persecutors of those who gloried in that cross!

We find earth-dwellers mentioned again in Revelation 8:13, immediately preceding the sounding of the last three trumpets. A loud voice declares: "Woe! Woe! Woe for those who dwell on the earth, because of the other voices of the trumpets of the three angels, who are yet to sound!"

Just before this, those who gave up pursuit of an earthly reputation and an earthly inheritance are seen, represented by the twenty-four royal priests, robed and crowned in heaven. Their theme of praise? The precious blood shed on the cross which had separated them from the world. What a terrible

---

[13] Rev. 3:10

[14] To be clear, these are ones that may have participated in Christendom, but never believed the gospel themselves; never trusted Christ alone for their personal salvation.

position they find themselves, those who refused the heavenly calling which, through grace, these people had learned to prize!

The earth that they had loved so faithfully is now the scene of the hardening judgments of God, and is fast slipping from their grasp. And they have lost all hope of heaven, though at one time, they fondly thought they might at least have a place there, when death should snatch them from their delights here. Hoping to have the best of both worlds, they have lost them both!

The testimony of God's "two witnesses"[15] only lacerates them into the agonies of despair. During the nearly universal joy over their deaths, when all the nations and peoples are celebrating in that awful day, we are told: "Those who dwell on the earth rejoice over them, and they will be glad. They will give gifts to one another, because these two prophets tormented those who dwell on the earth."[16]

But though no more prophetic voices proclaim their doom on earth, in heaven a loud voice cries, "Woe to the earth and to the sea, because the devil has gone down to you, having great wrath, knowing that he has but a short time."[17] Notice the stark contrast here, with the words immediately preceding: "Rejoice, heavens, and you who dwell in them."

In the next chapter, while authority is given to the Roman beast "over every tribe, people, language, and nation,"[18] yet it is specifically the earth-dwellers that worship him. For they will not be without a religion then, as they are not without one now. They are also referred to twice in Revelation 17, in connection with this same beast and its prostitute rider. "Those who dwell in the earth were made drunken with the wine of her sexual immorality."[19] "Those who dwell on the earth and whose names have not been written in the book of life from the foundation of the world will marvel when they see that the beast was, and is not, and shall be present."[20]

What a terrible outlook for apostate Christendom! It is the false Christ, the lamb-like beast, who leads them in their worship of the first beast. "He exercises all the authority of the

---

[15]Rev. 11:3   [16]Rev. 11:10   [17]Rev. 12:12   [18]Rev. 13:7   [19]Rev. 17:2   [20]Rev. 17:8

first beast in his presence. He makes the earth and those who dwell in it to worship the first beast, whose fatal wound was healed. He performs great signs, even making fire come down out of the sky to the earth in the sight of people. He deceives people who dwell on the earth because of the signs he was granted to do in front of the beast, saying to those who dwell on the earth that they should make an image to the beast who had the sword wound and lived."[21]

Such a strong delusion, God will give them up to! Those whose hearts were set on things down here now have a god and a christ of their own, of earth and suited to earth, but all alike soon to be destroyed at the appearing of the heavenly One in judgment.

In Revelation 14 we find the 144,000 of Israel distinguished from these as "those who had been redeemed out of the earth."[22] They are not the church, nor a part of it, but during the absence of "the Lamb" their hearts had gone out to Him in the place where He was and from where they waited expectantly for His coming, and thus they were not seduced by false Babylon or the Antichrist of the earth.

Immediately following this vision, we have the last word from God that the earth-dwellers will ever hear, until they meet the One they rejected in judgment. "I saw an angel flying in mid heaven, having an eternal Good News to proclaim to those who dwell on the earth, and to every nation, tribe, language, and people. He said with a loud voice, 'Fear the Lord, and give him glory; for the hour of his judgement has come. Worship him who made the heaven, the earth, the sea, and the springs of waters!'"[23] It is a call to end their wicked foolishness even though the hour is late, but we don't hear of any response from them.

Their dreadful doom as beast-worshipers is given in the message that follows: "he also will drink of the wine of the wrath of God, which is prepared unmixed in the cup of his anger."[24] Solemn words! The Lord Jesus drained a similar cup for sinners when He hung upon the cross, the truth of which

---

[21]Rev. 13:12–14   [22]Rev. 14:3   [23]Rev. 14:6,7   [24]Rev. 14:10

they had hated.   Now they must drink its fearful contents themselves.

Briefly then, this is the present and future path and portion of those who think about earthly things, "whose end is destruction." Let us see to it, beloved, that we walk in holy separation from them now, "hating even the clothing stained by the flesh." [25]

"If then you were raised together with Christ, seek the things that are above, where Christ is, seated on the right hand of God. Set your mind on the things that are above, not on the things that are on the earth. For you died, and your life is hidden with Christ in God." [26]

As foreigners and pilgrims, may it be our goal to press on in faith to the land where He has gone, who has won our hearts by dying for us on the cross, and who is soon coming to take us to be with Himself in the Father's house. How paltry and poor will Egypt's food look then, when we feast upon the hidden manna!

---

[25] Jude 1:23   [26] Col. 3:1–3

Jacob's Trouble and The Final Restoration

Jeremiah 30 and 31 are Bible passages which supply prophetic insight into Israel's earthly future. This is a revised excerpt of H.A. Ironside's commentary from 1906, and is included to provide further clarity on God's enduring plan for His chosen people.

NOWHERE in Scripture, as far as I am aware, do we have a clearer revelation relating to the final, literal restoration of Israel (preceded by the great tribulation) than in Jeremiah 30 and 31. If one studies these chapters along with Matthew 24, 25; Romans 11; and the books of Daniel and Revelation, it will help provide a clear outline of what God has in store for His earthly people. Because of its supreme importance in this regard, we will look at Jeremiah's revelation verse by verse.

> (30:1,2) The word that came to Jeremiah from the LORD, saying, "The LORD, the God of Israel, says, 'Write all the words that I have spoken to you in a book.

It is vitally important that we clearly understand the fact that here, as in all Scripture, God Himself is the One speaking. "Surely the Lord GOD will do nothing, unless he reveals his secret to his servants the prophets." [1] As He gives direction, the Lord specifically identifies himself with His people, so we can be sure that it is for our profit and blessing to seek to become acquainted with what is so obviously near to His heart.

---

[1] Amos 3:7

> (30:3) For, behold, the days come,' says the LORD, 'that I will reverse the captivity of my people Israel and Judah,' [2] says the LORD. 'I will cause them to return to the land that I gave to their fathers, and they will possess it.'"

We are told distinctly that both Israel *and* Judah (not only the latter) are to be returned to their land.

Their temporary restoration at the end of the seventy years of Babylonian exile does not fulfill the terms of this prophecy. When brought back to the home of their fathers, they are to "possess it," which was plainly not the case with those who returned under Zerubbabel, as their descendants were scattered again amongst the nations, and remain so to this day. [3]

Also at that time, though a few from the ten tribes went back with the remnant of Judah, there was no regathering of Israel, as such. When the Lord's appointed time to remember Zion has come, twelve thousand from each of the twelve tribes will be delivered out of the hand of the Gentiles. [4] It is possible that the number may be figurative, but it at least implies a significant company out of each tribe.

> (30:4) These are the words that the LORD spoke concerning Israel and concerning Judah.

Here again, note how clearly the northern and the southern kingdoms are referred to. Both have been scattered. Both are included in God's counsels of judgment and grace.

> (30:5) For the LORD says: "We have heard a voice of trembling; a voice of fear, and not of peace.

---

[2] Having divided into two kingdoms after Solomon, the ten tribes (forming the bulk of the nation) are distinguished as *'Israel'* while the tribes of Judah and Benjamin formed the kingdom of *'Judah.'*

[3] This chapter was originally written prior to 1948, and the establishment of the current state of Israel. Whether it is a modern fulfillment of this prophecy is debated amongst Christians, but regardless, it is not a complete fulfillment of all things prophecied in this chapter.

[4] See Rev. 7.

Before there can be the fulfillment of the promises of blessing, there must be the full tasting of the cup of the Lord's righteous indignation. Therefore, the subject these words introduce us to is that of *'the great tribulation.'*[5] Before the glorious appearing of Israel's once rejected Messiah and the establishment of His kingdom, the favoured nation will be exposed as never before to the power of the oppressor and to the malice of Satan. It is their special punishment for having crucified and killed the Anointed of the Lord.

> (30:6) Ask now, and see whether a man travails with child. Why do I see every man with his hands on his waist, as a woman in travail, and all faces are turned pale?

That time of trial will be so terrible (but so sure is the joy to follow) that it is likened to the labour pains that precede the birth of a child. Strong men will be in anguish just like a woman in her birth pangs.

> (30:7) Alas! for that day is great, so that none is like it. It is even the time of Jacob's trouble; but he will be saved out of it.

To the church, the promise is: "Because you kept my command to endure, I also will keep you from the hour of testing which is to come on the whole world, to test those who dwell on the earth."[6]

The saints of this present dispensation will be *kept from* the hour of testing. Those of the next period will be *saved out* of it—they will pass through it, but find deliverance at last when the Lord returns in glory. This short but dreadful time of sorrow is emphatically called the "time of Jacob's trouble." Although necessarily, others will be involved in it too.

In fact, all *'earth-dwellers,'*[7] will have to suffer while it continues on. But it is the special season of Israel's sifting, when God will repay them double for all their sins. Scripture gives no

---

[5]See Matt. 24:21 and Rev. 7:14.   [6]Rev. 3:10   [7]See further explanation in Appendix A.

hint of the church passing through this unparalleled tribulation. It is not for the testing of the members of the body of Christ, but for the chastisement of Israel.

> (30:8,9) It will come to pass in that day, says the LORD of Armies, that I will break his yoke from off your neck, and will burst your bonds. Strangers will no more make them their bondservants; but they will serve the LORD their God, and David their king, whom I will raise up to them.

The yoke referred to is that of the last great Gentile power, the ten-horned beast of Revelation 13—the Roman empire revived in its fearsome final form. The power of the beast will be destroyed by the appearing of the Lord Jesus Christ in flaming fire, with all the armies of heaven;[8] after which Israel, restored to their land, will enter into rest under the Messiah's kind and good rule. "David their king" no doubt refers, not to the first son of Jesse who wore the royal crown, but to the fact that the reign of the Lord is the fulfillment of the Lord's promise to raise up, in David's line,[9] One to rebuild his fallen tabernacle and to sit upon his throne.

"The Lord God will give him the throne of his father David, and he will reign over the house of Jacob forever. There will be no end to his Kingdom."[10]

This declaration, communicated by the angel Gabriel, has never been fulfilled in this present dispensation. Not for one moment has the Lord Jesus sat upon David's throne. He now sits upon His Father's throne (Revelation 3:21; Hebrews 1:3). At the end of this age He will rise from that throne, when His enemies are made His footstool (Hebrews 1:13; Psalms 110:1). Then He will descend to earth to fulfill the promise spoken of by Gabriel and all the prophets.

> (30:10) Therefore don't be afraid, O Jacob my servant, says the LORD. Don't be dismayed, Israel. For, behold, I will save

---

[8]See Rev. 17.   [9]See Rev. 22:16.   [10]Luke 1:32,33

you from afar, and save your offspring from the land of their
captivity. Jacob will return, and will be quiet and at ease. No
one will make him afraid.

Was this the case when the people of Judah returned by
permission of the Persian king Cyrus? Did they have peace and
quiet? Were they enjoying rest? Was no one made afraid?

The book of Nehemiah and the apocryphal records of the
Maccabees give the answer, as do the Gospels themselves. From
their return to the destruction of Jerusalem under Titus, we
have one long record of unrest and warfare. We must look
instead to the near future for the fulfillment of this prophetic
word.

(30:11) For I am with you, says the LORD, to save you; for I
will make a full end of all the nations where I have scattered
you, but I will not make a full end of you; but I will correct
you in measure, and will in no way leave you unpunished."

Their long-time dispersal amongst the Gentiles is the fulfillment
of this. The legend of the Wandering Jew, immortal, yet always
moving on, has its foundation here. It is impossible to destroy
the people whom the Lord has chosen! Empires may rise and fall,
nations may be wiped from existence, but Israel will survive, and
will triumph at last, ruling over all the earth.

(30:12-14) For the LORD says, "Your hurt is incurable. Your
wound is grievous. There is no one to plead your cause,
that you may be bound up. You have no healing medicines.
All your lovers have forgotten you. They don't seek you.
For I have wounded you with the wound of an enemy, with
the chastisement of a cruel one, for the greatness of your
iniquity, because your sins were increased.

Prophets and sages had tried in vain to promote healing. Even
disaster and captivity had not resulted in recovery. That the
spiritual wound was utterly incurable so far as human power

was concerned, the events at Calvary would soon make clear. God, in Christ, walked amongst them in lowly grace. Their response? They nailed Him to a cross. Therefore they must be, for a time, disowned by the Lord.

The Antichrist, the false shepherd, will rule over them in the day of their deepest tribulation. Their "lovers"—that is, the idols in which they had trusted—will do nothing to help them. They must come to fully understand that "it is a fearful thing to fall into the hands of the living God." [11]

The Gentile nations, however, who will be the agents inflicting the hurt, will in their turn, know the rod of the Lord's wrath. [12]

> (30:16) Therefore all those who devour you will be devoured. All your adversaries, everyone of them, will go into captivity. Those who plunder you will be plunder. I will make all who prey on you become prey.

Down through the centuries, the nations have been made to know the truth of this verse.

None who have oppressed Israel have prospered very long. Babylon and Assyria no longer exist; while Persia and Greece are still preserved. So too amongst modern nations. There should be no question that one source, at least, of the strength of Britain and the United states is found in this, that they have, as a general rule, befriended the Jews. On the other hand, the history of those powers who have stood against the Lord's people records disaster after disaster. Spain is witness to this; as, notably, is Russia also—that great dominion of Gog. [13]

> (30:17) For I will restore health to you, and I will heal you of your wounds," says the LORD; "because they have called you an outcast, saying, 'It is Zion, whom no man seeks after.'"

---

[11] Heb. 10:31   [12] See Lam. 3:1.   [13] See Ezek. 38.

Through the wounded One, the wounds of Israel will be healed, when, no longer outcasts, they will be called "Sought Out, A City Not Forsaken."[14]

(30:18-20) The LORD says: "Behold, I will reverse the captivity of Jacob's tents, and have compassion on his dwelling places. The city will be built on its own hill, and the palace will be inhabited in its own place. Thanksgiving will proceed out of them with the voice of those who make merry. I will multiply them, and they will not be few; I will also glorify them, and they will not be small. Their children also will be as before, and their congregation will be established before me. I will punish all who oppress them.

Earthly blessings await repentant Israel, just like they enjoyed before, when "there was no foreign god with him."[15]

The city, rebuilt upon the ancient site, will be filled with joy and gladness. Both young and elderly alike will be blessed, as Zechariah also prophesies:

"The LORD of Armies says: 'Old men and old women will again dwell in the streets of Jerusalem, every man with his staff in his hand for very age. The streets of the city will be full of boys and girls playing in its streets.'"[16]

They will no longer be oppressed by the arrogant stranger, but instead:

(30:21,22) Their prince will be one of them, and their ruler will proceed from amongst them. I will cause him to draw near, and he will approach me; for who is he who has had boldness to approach me?" says the LORD. "You shall be my people, and I will be your God.

There appears to be good reason to believe that the "prince" spoken of here is the same prince referred to so frequently in the last five chapters of Ezekiel.[17] He will, it appears, be a direct

---

[14]Isa. 62:12   [15]Deut. 32:12   [16]Zech. 8:4,5   [17]See Ezek. 44:3; 45:7; 46:2, etc.

lineal descendant of David, and will be the earthly ruler, subject in all things to the glorified Immanuel. In this day of the "restoration of all things, which God spoke long ago by the mouth of his holy prophets," [18] the hearts of the people will have been fully turned to the Lord—that is, the remnant He spares, for the apostate part of the nation will be destroyed in the great tribulation which is brought to our notice once more in the closing verses of this chapter.

> (30:23,24) Behold, the LORD's storm, his wrath, has gone out, a sweeping storm: it will burst on the head of the wicked. The fierce anger of the LORD will not return until he has accomplished, and until he has performed the intentions of his heart. In the latter days you will understand it."

The expression "the latter days" appears to be synonymous with "the time of the end" in Daniel 12, when "many will purify themselves, and make themselves white, and be refined; but the wicked will do wickedly; and none of the wicked will understand; but those who are wise will understand." [19]

The fury of the Lord will fall with awesome power upon the ungodly portion of the nation who embrace the Antichrist's wicked rule. But those who refuse *'the mark of the beast'* [20] and who honour the Lord's Word, will then come into blessing.

Jeremiah 31 continues on in the same general subject, with a particular focus on the deliverance of the righteous remnant, and the establishment of the New Covenant with them.

> (31:1) "At that time," says the LORD, "I will be the God of all the families of Israel, and they will be my people."

The Lo-Ammi [21] statement of Hosea 1:9 will be forever repealed, for it is written: "Yet the number of the children of Israel will be

---

[18] Acts 3:21   [19] Dan. 12:10   [20] See Rev. 13:16,17.   [21] Meaning, *'not my people.'*

as the sand of the sea, which can't be measured or counted; and it will come to pass that, in the place where it was said to them, 'You are not my people,' they will be called 'sons of the living God.'" [22]

(31:2) The LORD says, "The people who survive the sword found favour in the wilderness; even Israel, when I went to cause him to rest."

This no doubt refers to the faithful remnant in the latter day. By Ezekiel, a similar message is given:

"I will bring you out from the peoples, and will gather you out of the countries in which you are scattered with a mighty hand, with an outstretched arm, and with wrath poured out. I will bring you into the wilderness of the peoples *(or nations)*, and there I will enter into judgement with you face to face. Just as I entered into judgement with your fathers in the wilderness of the land of Egypt, so I will enter into judgement with you,' says the Lord GOD. 'I will cause you to pass under the rod, and I will bring you into the bond of the covenant. I will purge out from amongst you the rebels and those who disobey me. I will bring them out of the land where they live, but they shall not enter into the land of Israel. Then you will know that I am the LORD.'" [23]

In that unparalleled tribulation period, referred to in Matthew 24:21, the apostates of Israel will be destroyed by the judgment of the Lord. Following that, those who have faithfully walked in His ways will be established in the land.

All of this, however, is pure grace. It is God's own loving kindness that will attract their hearts to Himself. That is why we read next:

(31:3) The LORD appeared of old to me, saying, "Yes, I have loved you with an everlasting love. Therefore I have drawn you with loving kindness.

---

[22] Hos. 1:10   [23] Ezek. 20:34–38

It is His eternal love for them, not theirs for Him, that ensures their final blessing. So too with us Christian believers: "in this is love, not that we loved God, but that he loved us, and sent his Son as the atoning sacrifice for our sins."[24] When in us, as in Israel, there was absolutely nothing to draw out that love, except, of course, our deep and bitter need, He set His heart upon us and wooed us for Himself. He had dealt with His earthly people in this way; and having once set His affections on them, He will never give them up.

> (31:4) I will build you again, and you will be built, O virgin of Israel. You will again be adorned with your tambourines, and will go out in the dances of those who make merry.

For centuries, their harps have been hung up, on the willows, for "how can we sing the LORD's song in a foreign land?"[25] But soon that scene of dancing and singing led by Miriam on the banks of the Red Sea will be repeated on a grander scale, when all their enemies are overthrown forever. In that glad day of rejoicing and blessing, they will also enjoy bounty:

> (31:5) Again you will plant vineyards on the mountains of Samaria. The planters will plant, and will enjoy its fruit.

Jerusalem's temple will be rebuilt on a scale of magnificence previously unknown, and the twelve tribes will gather there again to celebrate the feasts of the Lord.

> (31:6,7) For there will be a day that the watchmen on the hills of Ephraim cry, 'Arise! Let's go up to Zion to the LORD our God.'" For the LORD says, "Sing with gladness for Jacob, and shout for the chief of the nations. Publish, praise, and say, 'The LORD, save your people, the remnant of Israel!'

---

[24] 1 John 4:10   [25] Psa. 137

The "time of the singing" described in Song of Solomon 2:12 will have truly come, when the Lord will again overturn the captivity of His people.

> (31:8,9) Behold, I will bring them from the north country, and gather them from the uttermost parts of the earth, along with the blind and the lame, the woman with child and her who travails with child together. They will return as a great company. They will come with weeping. I will lead them with petitions. I will cause them to walk by rivers of waters, in a straight way in which they won't stumble; for I am a father to Israel.   Ephraim is my firstborn.

God was not revealed as *'Father'* in an individual or personal sense in the Old Testament:

To Abraham, He was known as the *'All-Sufficient'*, or the *'Almighty'*;

To Moses, as the *'Lord'*; prophetically, as the *'Most High'*;

To the remnant in the days of Ezra and Nehemiah, as the *'God of heaven'*.

It was the Lord Jesus who revealed the Father to us—"my Father and your Father," [26] He says. This is blessedly individual. Each saint is a child, and can cry by the Spirit, "Abba, Father!" [27]

As a nation, Israel was His son. In recognizing them that way, He is spoken of as *'Father'*, but not in any nearer sense. "For you are our Father," the future remnant are entitled to say, "though Abraham doesn't know us, and Israel does not acknowledge us. You, LORD, are our Father. Our Redeemer from everlasting is your name." [28]

Earlier in the book of Jeremiah we notice the Lord's emotional appeal: "Will you not from this time cry to me, 'My Father, you are the guide of my youth!'?" [29]

---

[26]John 20:17   [27]Gal. 4:6. *'Abba'* is a Greek spelling for the Aramaic word for *'Father'* or *'Daddy'* used in a familiar, respectful, and loving way.   [28]Isa. 63:16   [29]Jer. 3:4

As a Father, often grieved but ever loving, He will rejoice over them when once more they ask the way to Zion.

(31:10) "Hear the LORD's word, you nations, and declare it in the distant islands. Say, 'He who scattered Israel will gather him, and keep him, as a shepherd does his flock.'

This is not a temporary restoration, not a gathering only to allow a scattering again. They will be brought back to be kept by the faithful "Shepherd of Israel," never again to wander from the fold.

(31:11) For the LORD has ransomed Jacob, and redeemed him from the hand of him who was stronger than he.

God has never given up His purpose of redemption. As a nation, they were sheltered by blood from judgment, and redeemed by power from Pharaoh's enslavement, when He brought them out of Egypt. He has contemplated them ever since from that standpoint.

His grace cannot allow any failure to bring them into the fullness of blessing at last, no matter how much their behaviour may have required Him to chastise them in the meantime. When brought safely through the time of Jacob's trouble, they will sing the song both of Moses and of the Lamb.[30] Their final deliverance is intimately connected with their salvation from bondage in the past.

(31:12–14) They will come and sing in the height of Zion, and will flow to the goodness of the LORD, to the grain, to the new wine, to the oil, and to the young of the flock and of the herd. Their soul will be as a watered garden. They will not sorrow any more at all. Then the virgin will rejoice in the dance; the young men and the old together; for I will turn their mourning into joy, and will comfort them, and make them rejoice from their sorrow. I will satiate the soul of the

---

[30] See Rev. 15.

priests with fatness, and my people will be satisfied with my goodness," says the LORD.

It is an utterly false system of exegesis [31] that would spiritualize all of this, and then apply it to the church in this dispensation. The language is plain and simple. It is a millennial picture, describing the joy of the Messiah's kingdom when established on the earth.

In Jeremiah 31:15–17 the tribulation period is referred to once more, with comforting assurances of eventual blessing. We know the words of Jeremiah 31:15 were used by the Holy Spirit in reference to the slaughter of the infants in Bethlehem, under Herod's cruel edict.

(31:15) The LORD says: "A voice is heard in Ramah, lamentation and bitter weeping, Rachel weeping for her children. She refuses to be comforted for her children, because they are no more."

Those horrible events in Matthew 2:16–18 are a similar case and an apt fulfillment of the passage. But the two following verses in Jeremiah make it evident that a second and more complete fulfillment is anticipated. It is distinctly stated that the children which Rachel is weeping over "will come again from the land of the enemy," [32] and that they "will come again to their own territory." [33] It is *captivity*, and not just slaughter, that is contemplated.

(This two-fold application of prophecy is very common in Scripture, for example, in Peter's quotation from the prophet Joel on the day of Pentecost. [34] The words will have a fuller fulfillment in the last days, as the kingdom is ushered in.)

From verses 18 to 21, the repentance of the ten tribes (often referred to under the name *'Ephraim'*, with the two other tribes

---

[31] *'Exegesis'* is the process of drawing out the meaning from a text in accordance with the context and intended meaning of its author. *'Eisegesis'* occurs when a reader imposes his or her interpretation into and onto the text. (Wikipedia)
[32] Jer. 31:16   [33] Jer. 31:17   [34] See Acts 2.

included in the term *'Judah'*) is vividly depicted.

> (31:18) "I have surely heard Ephraim grieving thus, 'You
> have chastised me, and I was chastised, as an untrained
> calf. Turn me, and I will be turned; for you are the LORD
> my God.

Hosea had declared: "Israel has behaved extremely stubbornly,
like a stubborn heifer." [35] This is Ephraim's own confession here,
but now they turn to the One so long refused and sinned against.
In true self-judgment Ephraim is heard to exclaim,

> (31:19) Surely after that I was turned. I repented. After that I
> was instructed. I struck my thigh. I was ashamed, yes, even
> confounded, because I bore the reproach of my youth.'

It is an acknowledgment of the Lord's grace in bringing them
back. Striking their thigh is, it would seem, an expression that
symbolizes entering once more into covenant. This re-turning
to God is draws an immediate response from the Lord, who
exclaims:

> (31:20) Is Ephraim my dear son? Is he a darling child? For as
> often as I speak against him, I still earnestly remember him.
> Therefore my heart yearns for him. I will surely have mercy
> on him," says the LORD.

The Lord will have them back. Thus the call to take the highway
back from the lands of the various nations to their ancestral home
in Palestine.

> (31:21) "Set up road signs. Make guideposts. Set your heart
> towards the highway, even the way by which you went.
> Turn again, virgin of Israel. Turn again to these your cities.

---

[35] Hos. 4:16

How boundless the grace that embraces as an undefiled *virgin*, the people that had been so horribly polluted!

> (31:22) How long will you go here and there, you backsliding daughter? For the LORD has created a new thing in the earth: a woman will encompass a man."

Many, including the so-called Church Fathers, apply this verse to the incarnation of Christ. The woman, they say, was the Virgin Mary; the man, her Holy Son. This interpretation however, seems to be quite out of context and a forced fit. Is it not more likely that the "woman" referred to is the "virgin of Israel" of the preceding verse? In that case, the "man" might possibly be the symbol of power in the hands of the Gentile.[36] Israel, in relative weakness as a woman, shall compass, or overcome, the power of the nations. An interpretation like this would harmonize better with the context. Admittedly, the verse is difficult to comprehend with confidence.

> (31:23-25) The LORD of Armies, the God of Israel, says: "Yet again they will use this speech in the land of Judah and in its cities, when I reverse their captivity: 'The LORD bless you, habitation of righteousness, mountain of holiness.' Judah and all its cities will dwell therein together, the farmers, and those who go about with flocks. For I have satiated the weary soul, and I have replenished every sorrowful soul."

At what time could Jerusalem have been referred to as the "habitation of righteousness" and the "mountain of holiness" in the five centuries following the return from exile by permission of King Cyrus? These are, beyond doubt, promises yet to be made good in the future. Note that they refer to *Judah*, not the church. Therefore the Jews must not only be brought back to their land, but also established there in the fear of the Lord, if

---

[36] See Nebuchadnezzar's dream in Dan. 2.

this prophetic word is to be carried out (and "Scripture can't be broken." [37])

Our prophet Jeremiah has been like a man in sleep while this vision of future glory and rest was unfolded to him. He wakes up and his heart is filled with a sweet, trusting peace as he realizes the purpose of GOD for his people.

(31:26) On this I awakened, and saw; and my sleep was sweet to me.

The following few verses recall the parable of the sour grapes spoken by Ezekiel at about the same time.

(31:27–30) "Behold, the days come," says the LORD, "that I will sow the house of Israel and the house of Judah with the seed of man and with the seed of animal. It will happen that, like as I have watched over them to pluck up and to break down and to overthrow and to destroy and to afflict, so I will watch over them to build and to plant," says the LORD. "In those days they will say no more, "'The fathers have eaten sour grapes, and the children's teeth are set on edge.' But everyone will die for his own iniquity. Every man who eats the sour grapes, his teeth will be set on edge.

In Ezekiel 18, we find that this proverb had become a common one on the lips of the people of Judah. Blind to their own sins, they attributed their misfortunes to the Lord's anger because of the evil actions of their fathers. This was far from being the case, as both Ezekiel and Jeremiah testify. Their *own* sins had resulted in the appropriate judgment. They had eaten the sour grapes, therefore their teeth were set on edge. "The soul who sins, he shall die." [38] They will be brought to confess this in the time of their greatest sorrow. As a result, we find the Lord sowing them once more in their land, building and planting, whereas before, He had been obliged to pluck up and afflict them.

---

[37] John 10:35   [38] Ezek. 18:20

Following this, the *new covenant* will be made with them. It is important to note that while we as Christians enjoy the blessings of the new covenant, it is never said to be made with the church. In the epistle to the Hebrews, as in the Jeremiah passage before us, it is distinctly stated that it is to be made with "with the house of Israel and with the house of Judah." [39]

The mediator of that new covenant is our Lord Jesus Christ. The blood of the new covenant is that blood which He shed for our sins.   Therefore, Christian believers now rejoice in the distinctive blessings it ensures, but it is with the earthly—not with the heavenly—people that the covenant itself is to be made.

> (31:31,32) "Behold, the days come," says the LORD, "that I will make a new covenant with the house of Israel, and with the house of Judah: not according to the covenant that I made with their fathers in the day that I took them by the hand to bring them out of the land of Egypt; which covenant of mine they broke, although I was a husband to them," says the LORD.

It is nonsensical to speak of a new covenant with the church when no former covenant had been made with us. However, in the case of Israel and Judah, it's different. They entered into the Mosaic covenant at Sinai. That covenant had two parties to it, and it was *conditional*. If they did their part in obedience, God would fulfill His by blessing.   On that basis, they sadly began forfeiting everything before the stone tablets were even brought down from the mountain top!   Legal righteousness: they had none.

In the new covenant, an *unconditional* covenant, God alone is the responsible One; they are placed in the position of recipients. It is pure grace.   As we too are saved by grace alone, it is clear that the same principle is operative in both cases.   But the new covenant as such, is in connection with them alone.

We see the terms of the covenant in the next two verses:

---

[39] Heb. 8:8–13

> (31:33,34) "But this is the covenant that I will make with the house of Israel after those days," says the LORD: "I will put my law in their inward parts, and I will write it in their heart. I will be their God, and they shall be my people. They will no longer each teach his neighbour, and every man teach his brother, saying, 'Know the LORD;' for they will all know me, from their least to their greatest," says the LORD: "for I will forgive their iniquity, and I will remember their sin no more."

Notice that there is no possibility of failure here, because all the pledges are on God's side! This covenant, therefore, once made, shall never be annulled. It is "an everlasting covenant, ordered in all things, and sure."[40] Israel and Judah, as one nation in the land—purged, repentant and forgiven—will never again forfeit the Lord's blessing. They will forever be debtors to His grace.

> (31:35–37) The LORD, who gives the sun for a light by day, and the ordinances of the moon and of the stars for a light by night, who stirs up the sea, so that its waves roar; the LORD of Armies is his name, says: "If these ordinances depart from before me," says the LORD, "then the offspring of Israel also will cease from being a nation before me forever." The LORD says: "If heaven above can be measured, and the foundations of the earth searched out beneath, then I will also cast off all the offspring of Israel for all that they have done," says the LORD.

The many who believe God has finished striving with Israel, and has permanently cast them off as His chosen people in favour of the church, somehow ignore this very clear promise from the very mouth of God Himself! One must deny the very existence of the sun, moon and stars to affirm that God is done with ethnic Israel. In the light of this passage, what possible basis is left for the promotion of *'replacement theology'* and teaching the ultimate rejection of the once-favored nation?

---

[40] 2 Sam. 23:5

Please also note: this is not a promise to bring Israel into blessing through the church, by incorporation into it. It is their national existence that is pledged, and their blessing as *Israelites* —not as Christians. They *must* be restored to their land, *must* be recognized once more as a nation, and *must* be brought into complete subjection to the Lord, embracing their once rejected Messiah as King and Saviour, otherwise the prophecies of this chapter collapse to the ground. Everything prophecied here is intensely literal.

Nothing could be more literal than the remaining verses, which need no further comment.

> (31:38-40) "Behold, the days come," says the LORD, "that the city will be built to the LORD from the tower of Hananel to the gate of the corner. The measuring line will go out further straight onward to the hill Gareb, and will turn towards Goah. The whole valley of the dead bodies and of the ashes, and all the fields to the brook Kidron, to the corner of the horse gate towards the east, will be holy to the LORD. It will not be plucked up or thrown down any more forever."

There is no past period of history that these words can be applied to. In our Lord's time, the filthy stench of the valley of Hinnom (with its dead bodies and ashes) still polluted the atmosphere. It was in no sense "holy to the Lord". It is only to the future we can look for a fulfillment that will align with, and transcend, the promise.

"The zeal of the LORD of Armies will perform this."[41]

---

[41] Isa. 9:7

www.ingramcontent.com/pod-product-compliance
Lightning Source LLC
Chambersburg PA
CBHW031627040426
42452CB00007B/711